THE ART OF PSYCHOLOGICAL WARFARE

The Ultimate Guide to Build Mental Toughness and Mind Control. Discover the Machiavelli Mindset to Master your Emotions and Mental Manipulation Using Self-Discipline

Kingsley Register

© Copyright 2020 by Kingsley Register - All rights reserved.

The content within this book may not be reproduced, duplicated or transmitted without direct written permission from the author or the publisher. Under no circumstances will any blame or legal responsibility be held against the publisher, or author, for any damages, reparation, or monetary loss due to the information contained within this book. Either directly or indirectly.

Legal Notice:

This book is copyright protected. This book is only for personal use. You cannot amend, distribute, sell, use, quote or paraphrase any part, or the content within this book, without the consent of the author or publisher.

Disclaimer Notice:

Please note the information contained within this document is for educational and entertainment purpose only. All effort has been executed to present accurate, up to date, and reliable, complete information. No warranties of any kind are declared or implied. Readers acknowledge that the author is not engaging in the rendering of legal, financial, medical or professional advice. The content within this book has been derived from various sources. Please consult a licensed professional before attempting any techniques outlined in this book.

By reading this document, the reader agrees that under no circumstances is the author responsible for any losses, direct or indirect, which are incurred as a result of the use of information contained within this document, including, but not limited to, errors, omissions, or inaccuracies.

Table of Contents

Introduction 1

Chapter 1: What is Psychological Warfare? 5

Chapter 2: War is Based on Deception - Principles of Sun Tzu 11

Chapter 3: The Manipulation 19

Chapter 4: Mental Control 28

Chapter 5: Why Genghis Khan is a Military Genius 32

Chapter 6: Do Whatever Is Needed - Machiavellian lessons 40

Chapter 7: People Moralism - Machiavelli 48

Chapter 8: The Power Potential within You 56

Chapter 9: Five Practices to Help You Be Your Best You 65

Chapter 10: Getting Started on Your 'Elite' Journey ... 73

Chapter 11: The Laying of Plans, Calculation and Estimation - Sun Tzu and Machiavelli 83

Chapter 12: The Principles of Time Management - Sun Tzu and Machiavelli 90

Chapter 13: Maintaining Dominance 97

Chapter 14: The Principle of Success & Happiness in Business & Life 105

Chapter 15: Psychological Strategies to give you an Advantage in Life 113

Chapter 16: The Difference between Persuasion and Manipulation 118

Chapter 17: Moral and Earn Respect 128

Chapter 18: Strategies to Improve Your Mental Toughness 135

Chapter 19: Be Calm and Strong in Every Situation .. 142

Conclusion 150

Introduction

Psychological warfare is not a type of mind control that a lot of people know about or even be aware is going on. But it is used in a lot of cases with governments and the military. Basically, this is a term that describes a specific action that is done in order to force a particular reaction in some other people.

In order to get this to work, the manipulator will need to go for a specific reaction. For example, during a war, the government might try to get the people behind them or a certain action by promoting how bad the other side is. When the government wants to get a bill passed in Congress, they might send out propaganda in the hopes of getting people to go for their cause. In most cases, people will not do their research, and they become manipulated without realizing it.

There are a lot of different techniques that can be used for this kind of mind control. The whole point, though, is to change the target audience's (this is a type of mind control that is usually done on a large group of people rather than on just one or two people at a time), behavior, reasoning, motives, emotions, beliefs, and value systems. The manipulator is going to use these techniques in order to either get a confession out of their victims or try to get them to behave and act in a way that is beneficial to the manipulators' objectives.

This tactic is not just used on those who are supposedly on the same side, such as the government and its citizens. It can also be used on enemies. Some groups will use the idea of psychological warfare in order to destroy any morale that their enemy has and even to depress the troops or people of the enemy to get a more favorable reaction.

Anyone can be a victim of psychological warfare. Some groups that can fit into this category include individuals, organizations, governments, and other groups. While this is most commonly recognized as a tactic used in the military, there is no reason to assume that it is only used in such circumstances.

So, let's take a look at how psychological warfare came about and why it can be so powerful when it comes to the various mind control techniques. In the early years, this was just a method of propaganda and not used as in depth as you might find it today. Some of the earliest chiefs and warlords recognized that it is important to use the tactic of terror in order to scare away any of their opponents. One person who is believed to have used this tactic is Alexander the Great while he was conquering the Middle East and Europe. Many people believe that without this kind of mind control, the people he conquered would have risen up and he would never have had the power he was able to control. But since he instilled fear into those he took over and used this tactic to his advantage, he was successful.

Not only was Alexander the Great able to use terror to frighten the people when he took over, he also made sure that his own culture was going to be accepted by the people. He left some men from his military in each city that they conquered and he charged these men with oppressing any views that went against their new leader, introducing Greek language and culture, and even to marry the locals to help with assimilation.

Another group that may have used this tactic is Genghis Khan. During the time that he was taking over a lot of lands, just his name was enough to send terror through the masses. Those who had been captured worked hard to toe the line while those who were still free were worried that he would come and take them over as well. This was mostly because the Khan were not friendly to those who fought against them. It was not uncommon for them to kill many who got in their way and perform many acts of terror during their reign. This news would quickly spread out through word of mouth to other areas and people were afraid to get on the wrong side.

It was not just during the ancient past that psychological warfare was used; in fact, it has been used more now in modern times than it ever was in the past. World War II is a great example of how this kind of mind control was used since so many different countries all used it.

Think about how much Germany was able to take over the rest of the world. When they first started out with their campaign, they were a small nation that was still beaten down after the end of World War I. But somehow, they were able to take over a large part of Europe and all of the countries who were still free were terrified and begging for the U.S. to come to help them. How was Hitler able to make such a splash in this large area?

Many believe that he used psychological warfare to get his point. In fact, there is very little fighting done between Germany and the countries that it takes over. Outside of the first few countries, Germany many times was able to just walk into a country and take it over, even with England and France right there and easily able to take over. This is because the countries in this area were very scared of Hitler and the terror he was sending around. Thanks to his own personal propaganda that was sent out to the other countries and other words of mouth tactics, Hitler was basically able to run over some other, much bigger countries, to get exactly what he wanted.

Chapter 1: What is Psychological Warfare?

Psychological warfare is the more mental side of the war. It is very insidious, both because of its high level of power, and because of its subtlety. Many people do not realize that they have been victims of psychological wars until they learn the signs and techniques. Psychological warfare involves using subtle methods to influence or alter someone's beliefs, feelings, and behavior, thus gaining control over someone from a distance. When you are in control of a person's mental and physical processes, you have tremendous power over the person. You can influence someone to do whatever suits your needs.

Psychological warfare uses a large variety of techniques to subdue the enemy. You can use light and sound to cause subliminal effects on your enemy's mind. You can use propaganda, rumors, and other forms of public communication to influence someone's decisions. You can ruin a person's reputation and confidence. Through a variety of physical, mental, and emotional means, you can gain control over someone and ruin someone's life. The fine techniques of psychological warfare are covered in more detail in the next phase.

Psychological warfare is typically far more effective than any other form of attack. Not only are you able to remain totally undetected, but you can also cause true harm. There are no laws against psychological warfare.

There are other names for psychological warfare. These include PSYOP (Psychological Operations), heart and mind, propaganda, political warfare, and MISO (Military Information Support Operations). These names give you a hint that psychological warfare is a favorite operation employed by the military. Governments use psychological warfare in war and intelligence because it is very effective and very covert.

Real Life Applications

There are four common uses of psychological warfare. First, this can be used to influence foreign people and governments to take stances that are friendly to the invading government. For instance, the United States could convince the people of an African nation to hate their own government. The people start a revolution, which breaks down the government. The United States can then easily invade the country, using the guise that they are providing "aid" and taking advantage of the fact that the military is too preoccupied with the revolution to stave off the invasion.

Second, psychological warfare involves strategic spats of terror to control a population. Acts of random violence, espionage, and other methods put people in a constant state of anxiety and fear.

People are thus more likely to accept anything in order to gain some sort of relief. A government or dictator can easily take advantage of a situation where people are terrified, just by promising people safety.

Third, brainwashing, hypnosis, and other forms of mind control and manipulation are employed to change others' personalities and viewpoints. People become tools and are changed or altered against their own wills. The government and the media can work together to change the general opinions of its people.

Finally, psychological warfare can be used to mold the general attitudes of entire populations. A classic example of this is how American people were molded to hate terrorists, without entirely understanding just who or what the enemy was. What exactly are terrorists? Are they Muslim extremists, or do they include other groups of people? Governments use this modeling to drive public opinion and gain the support needed for war. Governments can influence their own people to support a cause, when the government really has a secret agenda. Referring to the terrorist example, it is theorized that the American hatred of the terrorist was used by the US government to garner public support for an oil war in the Middle East. While this is certainly a matter of opinion, it is an example of how a government can earn its people's support for a public agenda, when really it has an entirely different, secret reason for wanting war.

All of these methods are used by governments in real life. However, you can adapt them for personal use. People can and do adapt government psychological warfare methods all the time for their own personal agendas.

You can use troublemaking and instigating tactics to turn people against each other or their idols. You can undo their personal beliefs. By disabling the social supports and belief systems of people, you can disable everything that gives them strength. People will fall into chaos without the frameworks that they have created for their own minds.

You can use terror to subdue people. When your enemies are scared, you have the ultimate power. You can offer them relief if they do something for you, or you can coerce them with threats. Fear is a powerful motivator.

You can also change peoples' personalities to suit your desires. You can brainwash people to become automatons at your mercy. Over time, you can get them to abandon beliefs and values that go against your personal ends. In the end, you will have the ultimate emotional and mental slave.

Covertly, you can get people to root for causes and unintentionally serve secret agendas that you have. For instance, you can get people to donate to your charity by convincing them that you support a cause that they are passionate about. What people don't know is that your charity is actually set up in order to grant tax benefits for a politician.

Media and news companies are often guilty of employing psychological warfare. Presidential campaign coverage is an example of how media outlets try to use psychological warfare techniques, such as propaganda, to influence people to vote for a certain candidate. Tom Brokaw is one news anchor who was accused of subliminally influencing people to vote for certain Republican candidates every year. Without intending to influence people, Brokaw would dedicate a certain enthusiasm to the candidates he liked, unintentionally spinning these candidates in a more appealing light. His viewers, who were already primarily Republican, were thus even more influence to vote for these candidates after watching his broadcasts.

Most people are still unaware of the nuances of psychological warfare. That is partly what makes it so useful. It is largely covert, so enemies are caught unaware and unprepared. They do not even know that their government or another individual is attacking them. Rather, people only feel that they are being goaded into doing what is right. They become excited and loyal to causes without understanding the hidden motives that lie behind these causes. The deliberate misdirection of people is a clever and almost foolproof way to influence people psychologically to serve your own personal ends.

The government uses psychological warfare to gain control over its citizens and other countries' citizens. But you can use psychological warfare to gain control over the people in your life. The home use of psychological warfare is similar to the military's use of it, but your purpose is probably either to get your way or to hurt someone close to you. You can adapt the methods employed by the government to make psychological warfare work for you in a personal setting.

There are many personal benefits to psychological warfare. Using the second guessing, manipulation, deception, persuasion, and torture advice contained in this phase, you can achieve whatever you want. You can psychologically hurt people until they are no longer threats to you. You can manipulate and persuade people to give you whatever you want. You can even make people want to date you or befriend you because of your power over them. People will become your enemies or your allies, and everyone will fear you and respect your wishes.

Read on to find out the ways to adapt government methods in order to use psychological warfare to your personal advantage.

Chapter 2: War is Based on Deception - Principles of Sun Tzu

Sun Tzu said: When an army is first to the battlefield it will be fresh and ready for fighting. The army that comes second will rush to get into place and will be exhausted.

Before you take on a new task or project, make sure you set yourself up to be successful at it.

Stay alert by relaxing and sleeping well.

Strengthen your body by eating well and exercising.

Strengthen your mind and spirit by reading motivational books and biographies of successful people. Listen to motivational speakers each morning.

Plan well and be prepared for the next step on your journey.

Sun Tzu said: A clever fighter will put his will onto his enemy but will not allow the enemy to do the same to him.

It is not necessary to fight every battle that comes your way. Fight only the battles you can win on your terms.

Pass up or retreat from a situation that is not favorable. Choose your battles.

Larry was always of slight physical build and poor at sports, but he was always good at talking and making people laugh. Larry didn't try out for sports and instead made his way through college by being the funny guy. His personality got him all the attention he needed.

Ted couldn't compete with the chain fast food joints in his hometown but he could still succeed by selling his homemade baked authentic pizzas.

Janet couldn't compete with the large venture capital firms that poured millions of dollars into new technology start-ups, so she focused her efforts on providing investment capital and a hands-on approach to small boutique businesses run by individual fashion designers.

Sun Tzu Said: When marching through a territory that has no enemy the soldiers will be able to move great distances without any problems.

Keep an eye out for new and unexplored markets or opportunities and step in to fill a need the same way so many famous pioneers and innovators have done in the past.

Then consider the self-belief those pioneers and innovators needed to be successful.

Moving through uncharted territory requires immense self-belief because there are no sign posts and no one to follow. But the best opportunities can be found in such territory, and its lack of limits allows much distance to be covered at a very fast pace.

Sun Tzu said: If you attack places that are undefended then you can be sure of victory and success. Likewise, you would be wise to build your defenses so they are in an unassailable position.

The world is always evolving and presenting new opportunities and frontiers. It is the ability to take on those undefined areas that provide us with a rich reward.

Sun Tzu said: The art of war requires knowledge of subtlety and secrecy; if you can master these skills then the enemy's fate is in your hands.

When you first find these new and unexplored places, your first instinct may be to rush off excited and tell everyone you know about your new find. Keep your ideas under wraps. Patent them and draw up a business plan. Take the next steps you need to make your dream a reality.

Sun Tzu: If you target and strike at the enemy's weak points then you will be able to gain a great victory, and if you are swifter than him then you will always be out of harm's way.

Sometimes the best way to get the most out of a new idea is to move quickly with it. If you spot a gap in the market then you have to move quickly in order to capitalize on it before others do.

The difference between moving quickly and moving slowly can be measured in the cost of millions of dollars of lost revenue or in ultimate victory.

Sun Tzu said: If we are trying to avoid engaging in battle then we must look to put something unusual and peculiar in the enemy's way. This will make him stop and question the battlefield and this new variable.

The art of bluffing is one of the most useful skills that one can have. It is so useful even Mother Nature uses it. The pufferfish has a slow locomotion but compensates with blowing itself up and making itself appear several times bigger while also becoming a spiky ball. This is to warn off others, but should another creature call a puffer fish's bluff it will find the spiky ball contains a toxin that can kill.

Bluffing can be a wonderful tool to get you out of a very tricky spot. When used correctly it can give you a significant advantage either in your personal, business, or investment life. But it's a skill that has to be practiced to perfection as it only works well when done well.

Sun Tzu said: If we are able to create a cohesive force, while we cause the enemy to split up, we will be able to conquer him.

Divide and conquer. No matter how big or powerful a system is when divided it can be easily overcome. Consider a system's weakest link and attack it. Even a seemingly unbreakable force can be damaged via such a strategy.

Sun Tzu said: We should keep the time and location of the engagement hidden from the enemy. This will mean the enemy will need to divide his force across several fronts. This will mean he is thinly spread across his borders.

Plans that remain secret will be extremely effective as you will be able to keep your enemy guessing your next move. This will also give you time to think about your own strategy.

Manage your information flow well. The more you know about your competitors' plans the greater the advantage you have over them. The less you know about them then the lower the chance you have of success if you attack them.

Guard your own information as it can mean the difference between your competitor challenging you or leaving you alone while he tries to predict your next move.

Sun Tzu Said: Probe the opposing force for its strengths and weaknesses. Then look at your own strengths and weaknesses and compare the two.

Gauge your strengths and weaknesses against the task at hand.

The balance of victory is not absolute but is a relative measure. What works in one situation may not work in another; there is no one solution fits all.

Sun Tzu Said: Everyone can see results and how the battle was won but none can see the strategy out of which victory is evolved.

Some successful people are like ducks that look calm and collected as they float majestically on a lake. But if you were to look underneath the surface you would see their little legs paddling furiously to keep them moving.

You do not need to show people your plans and brag about how many hours you have toiled. Just keep moving.

Sun Tzu said: Do not reuse the same tactics which have won one victory, but instead look to varying them accordingly.

You cannot expect to always use the same skill or strategy through life because the world is always changing. You are better off if you keep moving and going onto bigger and better things.

Take on situations and tasks on your own terms rather than someone else's. Don't let market forces or other people push you around.

Stay in flux and take on new projects and tasks when they suit you, i.e., when things are most favorable for you to be successful.

Sun Tzu said: Strategic tactics are like water, which runs from high places to low places. Avoid what is strong; you should strike at what is weak.

Take the path of least resistance as you remain focused on your goal, not on various problems you encounter along the way. Deal with those problems effectively and move on.

Sun Tzu said: Just as water is in no constant shape, so in warfare there are no constant conditions. Modify your tactics in relation to your enemy.

By focusing on the goal and looking for solutions you can find ways to reach your goal given the resources that you have. Sometimes the solution is sitting in front of you but if you don't place your awareness in that direction, you won't see it as the way forward.

Remain aware that the conditions in which you work are constantly changing and adapt your tactics accordingly. Keep learning and upgrading your skills to meet the needs of the marketplace.

Sun Tzu said: The five elements (water, fire, wood, metal, earth) are not found in equal measure; like the changing seasons each one will have its turn to be predominant. There are hot days and cold days and the moon has its cycles.

Everyone has a different set of personal attributes. While some people are physically strong, others are smart with numbers and others are musical and others insightful.

Some people start with more money, better connections, and better communities with better resources such as transportation, schools, and jobs.

We all, however, have been given the gift of self-determination—we can choose to make the most of what we have and work towards being successful in whatever we do.

Chapter 3: The Manipulation

Manipulation is the art of subtly influencing people to do what you want. It grants you control over people mentally and emotionally. Using a variety of subtle techniques, you can gain vast power over the minds of others. You can then use this power to your advantage.

Manipulation is undoubtedly one of the best tools for getting your way. People are not always willing to do your bidding. You do not have to accept no for an answer, however. You can simply use manipulation to ensure your success. Get people to inadvertently do what you want.

You can also use manipulation as a means to hurt and mentally break people. By weaving a tight web of negative emotions around someone, emotions such as fear and inadequacy, you can cripple someone's will. People will become reliant on you for their emotional well-being. They will also begin to doubt their sanity.

Manipulation is one of the main cornerstones of psychological warfare. You cannot perform psychological warfare if you do not know how to gain control over someone's mind. This is your guide to gaining this subtle yet powerful control.

FOG

When using manipulation, use a combination of fear, obligation, and guilt to create an emotional web that will trap a person. Inject fear into him. Then act sweet, so that he feels obligated to help you. If he ever goes against your wishes, use guilt to make him feel terrible. You can even hurt yourself to get him to stay and serve you longer.

These three emotions are essential when you are using psychological warfare. You want to keep someone in a constant state of one of these three emotions in order to exert control. Known as FOG, these emotions literally create a fog over someone's judgment.

Conceal Your Intent as Goodwill

To successfully manipulate a person, you must take care to disguise your true intentions. Nobody will want to do anything for you if they know that you are up to no good. Therefore, you must conceal your intent as goodwill. Make people believe that you mean the best. Show people that you care and that you are simply looking out for them. Do good and kind things to make it seem like you are just a Good Samaritan. In reality, you are just doing things to ingratiate yourself with your victims. But no one has to know this.

Making Someone an Offer that they can't refuse

When you want to gain control over someone, you must make him want to give you control. The best way to do this is to offer something that he really wants. This could be money, security, or love. This could be flattery and ego boosting. Most people do want to be loved, so you can often use affection and the promise of unconditional love as a means to gain control over people. Sex is also often a powerful motivator for human behavior and offering good sex is a tantalizing offer that many people will not be able to refuse. The reason that sex and love work so well is because they boost a person's self-esteem. A person relies on self-esteem to feel good. If you always make someone feel good, then he will want to come back to you for more. He will do anything to please you so that he can keep getting this sensation of being loved and wanted from you.

It is important to read a person to learn what he really desires. If he mentions that he wants someone to help him stop feeling so lonely, be that person who makes him not feel lonely. If he mentions that he just wants money, offer him money-making opportunities that will help him exponentially.

Power of Suggestion

The power of suggestion is just that, a power. The things you say to someone can really have a great bearing on their psyche. By making certain suggestions, you can manipulate someone into thinking exactly what you want him to think.

The power of suggestion works on changing someone's self-concept. Through a few small, meaningful hints, you can make someone doubt his self-concept. He will start to wonder if there is truth to what you have said. He may begin to believe you, especially if life continues to reinforce the words that you have uttered.

You can tell someone that he will never be a good father. He will thus develop doubt and insecurity about his fatherhood. Each of his normal failures in parenthood will act to reinforce this belief, until he has absolutely no faith in his capability as a dad. His beliefs will become a self-fulfilling prophecy.

Exploit Fear

The flip side to promising someone what they want is to threaten them with what they fear the most. You can exploit someone's fears and insecurities to gain control over him. Listen to what someone says to find out what scares him the most, and you have some very pertinent information about someone. You have a weakness that you can now exploit.

There are two ways that you can use someone's own fear against him. The first way is to threaten someone with what he fears the most to keep him from leaving the safety of your affection. If someone fears ageing, for instance, you can claim that he will grow old alone if he ever leaves you. You can point out his wrinkles or his few gray hairs all the time, so that he feels old and believes that no one will want to be with him now. As a result, he will stay with you and tolerate your manipulation.

Another use of someone's fear is when you want to influence someone. If you do not want someone to do something, for instance, use his fear of failure to convince him that he will fail so he will not try anything. Threaten someone with his own fears to make him submit to your will.

You can make someone feel unsafe in his own home as a form of psychological warfare. Use the power of fear to manipulate someone by telling him horror stories about the neighborhood or about electric fires and other catastrophes. You can make him so fearful that he will be more likely to do your bidding. He may even move away.

Emotional Blackmail

Emotional blackmail uses the fear, obligation, and guilt that are required to successfully manipulate someone. You basically use fear, obligation, and guilt to make someone feel like they owe you and they must do what you want. Should someone fail to do what you want, you can threaten to hurt him or the ones he loves, badly.

You can use all sorts of threats. Read a person well to determine what threats will work. Usually, threats of withdrawing love work the best. Threats against someone's family are also usually highly successful. You can use what he cares about as a bargaining tool or a threatening device.

Psychological warfare can also use literal blackmail. If some sort of truth would hurt someone should it leak, then you can use that truth as a means to get your way. "I will tell everyone about..." is a good threat to hold over someone's head. Make sure to gain as much information about people as you can. The threat of blackmail will make them scramble to do your bidding.

Passive-Aggressive Behavior

Passive-aggressive behavior allows you to act aggressively, without getting caught. You act in a way that makes others find it impossible to confront you for any specific behavior. Nevertheless, you are still able to express aggression and create a lingering fear of your anger. Passive-aggressive behavior is sneaky and non-direct.

You can use all sorts of indirect methods to express your anger and hostility. You can sulk and act sullen, you can refuse to do tasks, and you can conveniently "forget" about important things, such as birthdays. You can also leave passive aggressive notes or messages that say things like, "I worked really hard on this so it would be nice if everyone respected what I did." Making snide comments designed to hurt someone, without actually insulting them, is another way to be passive-aggressive. You might dismiss someone's hard work or someone's feelings. You can pretend to compliment someone, when really you are insulting them. Basically, you want to always mask your anger.

Gossiping

Gossiping is one of the most essential weapons of psychological warfare. Just as the military has certain kinds of guns, you must have certain weapons. Gossiping is one that you are required to have. Gossiping enables you to accomplish two things: discredit someone and make someone intensely uncomfortable.

By spreading stories about someone, you can get everyone to hate him. You can create a negative, uncomfortable environment of hostility. No one likes to know that others are talking about them without their knowledge. It creates a sense of paranoia and unhappiness. Use this to your advantage to make an environment practically unbearable to someone with clandestine gossip.

You can also make it clear to someone that you are not happy with him without telling him yourself. Other people will tell him for you. He will change his actions after hearing about the horrible things that you have been saying about him behind his back. You never have to say a word. This is a form of passive aggressive behavior.

Changing the Energy of a Room

You can change the energy of a room by being sulky, embarrassing, or dramatic. You're horrible, childish behavior will make the person that you are trying to manipulate feel so uncomfortable that he will do anything just to get you to stop. You can also make the situation that he is in so unbearable that he will leave.

Many kids employ this on their parents by screaming and crying when they are bored. They know that their parents will get uncomfortable and leave to comfort them. You can behave childishly too and it will probably work. For instance, if someone wants to go to a party, you can come along, but act like a baby and pout the whole time. You will drag the mood of the party down so low that your companion will probably leave just to get you to stop being so ugly.

But be aware that this can damage your own reputation. Other people will think less of you if you act like a child.

Keep the Focus on the Other Person

No one likes to just sit there listening to you talk about yourself. People prefer to go on and on about themselves. Therefore, you can get someone to like you by letting them talk about themselves ceaselessly. Ask them questions to show your fake interest, and pretend to hang on their every word. People will think that you are wonderful. You want to maintain this wonderful, selfless image when running manipulation on anyone. You will seem like the most dazzling person in the room.

In addition, you can glean a lot of information about people when you let them talk. You can find out fears and likes they have that you can later exploit if you need them. Pay careful attention to people when they talk to you. You never know what could be a useful weapon later on.

Chapter 4: Mental Control

There are tips that you can use to guard yourself against mind control (and break free). There are different strategies of mind control, but neuron-linguistic programming or NLP, mind control is a popular version that has been used by everyone from self-help gurus and coaches to politicians and other prominent people in the public eye. These types of mind control have been described previously, but it involves using language to induce a trance-like state, even vague language. You can break free from NLP mind control and you can protect yourself. Here are some tips.

Tip 1. Avert your eyes and move them about unpredictably

Eye contact is a very powerful way to make an emotional connection with someone. Even animals engage in this to some degree. A great way to confuse some controlling you is to move your eyes around in a way that it is unpredictable. This prevents them from using eye contact as a means of inducing control and it also will trip them up and make them uncomfortable.

Tip 2. Be suspicious of the use of nonspecific language

It is fascinating to learn the techniques of mind control as some of them are so simple. Vague language has been shown to be effective at controlling the thoughts and motivations of others. In particular, public speeches that use vague language can induce a sort of group trance. Any sort of language that is nonspecific that you hear from a potential manipulator or narcissist should be a red flag.

Tip 3. Pay attention

Someone using mind control techniques will be closely attuned to any lack of attention on your part and that may be a cue for them to try some mind control. Be aware of the sorts of things that are said to you when you appear not to be paying attention, or just pay closer attention in the future.

Tip 4. Stop letting other people touch you

We talked about touching in terms of manipulation, but it applies here as well. In this case, the touching is not actually to influence you but maybe to put you into a trance. Another touch later can be enough to bring you out of a trance or to put you back in if you are already out. Breaking free from mind control can be as simple as not allowing others to touch you.

Tip 5. Be cautious of someone speaking without really saying anything

Part of what makes hypnosis as alarming as that there are tricks that hypnotists use to induce a trance in the listener. There are certain words or types of words that can induce this state so it is important to be suspicious of people who are speaking in ways that sound like gibberish to you. The idea here is not that the words have no meaning at all, but that they seem to be saying something but that the words have little meaning when taken together. Think typical political speech.

Tip 6. Be suspicious of what others are really saying

Speech is the tool that hypnotists use to control you so you must pay attention to what they are saying and what the words indicate to break free. Someone trained in NLP may make a statement but thrown in there may be words that can be taken differently. Those may be suggestions that have been hidden amongst another language. Be aware of the ways that NLP practitioners suggest things to you.

Tip 7. Leave situations where you feel that you are being guided into a decision

Sometimes the best step to breaking free from mind control is getting away from the situation. NLP practitioners are skilled enough that they can control you through suggestions and other tactics while you are entirely clueless about the situation. If you find that you are being guided into action or decision it may be a good idea to simply leave. This is sort of like closing the door on the Jehovah's Witness, but sometimes that is what you have to do.

Tip 8. Let your intuition about people guide you

Sometimes your intuition about people is right, especially when it comes to behaviors that you observe that appear strange. This is sort of like the scene in The Matrix where Neo sees the same cat twice and his crew tells him that this is a sign that the agents changed something. If you see something or hear something that seems or looks strange to you, it probably is.

Tip 9. Be suspicious of language that allows you to engage in a behavior

You may think that a narcissist or manipulator will engage in language that orders you to do this or that, but this is not how neuro-language programming works. They use calming, permissive language to induce you to go into a trance. Commands are not effective in the manner that permissive language is so on the lookout for this.

Tip 10. Do not permit others to copy your body language

Part of what alarms about mind control is that it works because human beings are susceptible to mind control. Indeed, you cannot even call it being clueless because most people simply do not know what is going on. Someone copying your body language can be a sign that they are engaged in mind control so one step towards breaking this pattern is immediately aware of this and sensing danger.

Chapter 5: Why Genghis Khan is a Military Genius

Genghis Khan's early success and the rapid expansion of his Mongol Empire was largely a result of his military acumen. The Mongol armies were different from anything the world had seen before. They were organized differently, they fought differently, and they had different ideas. The generals placed in positions of command by Genghis Khan were men who had earned their power rather than men from a particular family. By giving important military roles to those who were most deserving, Genghis had ensured that his armies were led by intelligent men who would have the skills to adapt to circumstances and learn from experience.

As the Mongol Empire spread across Central Asia, the Mongol armies were able to take advantage of the technology and innovative techniques employed by the people they conquered. As they gained experience of many types of warfare, they were able to develop strategies that would work against any enemy they encountered.

Military Strategy

Genghis Khan was undoubtedly a great military strategist. He took into consideration what the enemy was thinking, basing his actions on how he anticipated the enemy would react. While there are plenty of stories that suggest he acted in anger, retaliating for insults and taking disproportionate vengeance, there is no suggestion that this anger led him to make irrational decisions. In fact, all of his military campaigns were very much based on logic, strategy, and thorough knowledge of his enemies' motivations. Battle strategy was a priority for Genghis, and he developed plans of attack that were often extremely complicated. For each battle, he would carefully weigh the risks and potential gains of engaging with the enemy before he attacked. He was not afraid to withdraw if he felt the risks outweighed the benefits and would hold back until he could be reasonably sure of victory. While he was by all accounts a brave fighter, Genghis himself would often withdraw and hide from the battle itself. He had a personal guard of 10,000 elite soldiers to protect him, but his role as the leader of the Mongol Empire and the motivating force of the armies made him a prize target and too precious a leader to risk losing in battle.

Intelligence and Espionage

One of the ways that Genghis ensured that he was making good strategic choices was by establishing a network of spies who gathered intelligence that would help guide his battle tactics. These spies were sent into an area in disguise to create maps that would show travel routes and useful resources as well as taking note of defenses and any other relevant inside information. This intelligence could be passed on quickly using a fast relay messenger system.

Genghis' spies also served another purpose. Disguised as travelers or traders, they were able to tell the local people tales of where they had been and what they had seen. This was an ideal opportunity to spread terrifying stories about the Mongol forces in order to create fear and unease within the population. Exaggerated stories about the atrocities committed or heroic tales about cities who had submitted and been treated with mercy by the Mongols could quickly spread through a community, and this had a profound effect on how the local people saw the Mongols and thus how they reacted when the Mongols approached.

Loyal Soldiers

The soldiers themselves were a highly organized and disciplined force. Every man in the Mongol Empire was automatically a soldier; there was little choice in the matter. The soldiers were intensively trained in horsemanship, weaponry, and battle tactics. Genghis used a massive annual hunting festival to train the soldiers, which was why hunting of certain animals was forbidden during the breeding season to allow greater numbers of animals for this annual hunt.

Perhaps the most important quality in a soldier, in the eyes of the universal leader, was loyalty. Genghis demanded absolute loyalty from his soldiers, and he achieved it through a mixture of fear—disloyalty was punishable by death—and incentive—loyalty was rewarded. In return for loyal service, soldiers were given a share of the bounty from looted enemy settlements, and they were treated relatively well. The armies were well supplied by a complex supply system that kept them well-fed and armed. Spiritual guidance and medical attention were provided by shamans who accompanied the army. Family life was entirely possible, with huge caravans of nomadic families following the armies.

The Cavalry

The key to understanding the Mongol army and how it differed to other armies of the time lies in understanding the role of the cavalry. The Mongol army was mostly made up of cavalry, but instead of the heavy cavalry seen in other armies such as the European knights, the majority of these were light cavalry who relied upon speed, mobility, and excellent archery skills to rain down arrows on the enemy and quickly change direction to evade an attack.

The Mongol light cavalry was highly trained in complex maneuvers. They used stirrups and gripped the horse with their legs so that they could fire arrows while riding at full speed. They were famed for their ability to fire arrows in all directions, including behind them. These soldiers were expert archers, timing each shot to precisely the split second when all four of the horses' legs were off the ground to get a smooth shot.

The horses used by the Mongols were exceptionally well suited to life in the Mongol army, and the success of the Mongol Empire owed a lot to the small but perfectly formed Mongol horse. Mongol horses were happy to graze and forage, so no grain was needed to feed them, making it easier to travel long journeys without the need for supplies. They were hardy and could handle low temperatures, which gave the Mongols an advantage when fighting in tough conditions during winter, especially in Russia. Each soldier had a number of horses so he could always be sure of having a fresh, healthy horse on long journeys or when faced with unexpected combat.

Horses held an almost sacred role in Mongol life. They were protected by extensive armor, and when a soldier died, it was not uncommon for his horse to be sacrificed so that they would remain together in the hereafter.

Contrary to popular belief, nearly four out of ten Mongol soldiers were heavy cavalry. Heavy cavalry generally carried lances and blades, which allowed them to attack in close combat after the light cavalry archers had broken up the enemy's lines of defense. The combination of a highly mobile light cavalry and a well-armed heavy cavalry behind proved to be deadly.

Decimal Military Divisions

Genghis revolutionized how armies were divided up. Instead of forming armies based on the status or tribe of the soldiers, he had very strict ideas about how an army should be formed. Units of ten men were formed. These were known as an arban, and they contained men from different tribal backgrounds and of different social status. A company of one hundred men was known as a jaghun, one thousand men formed a mingghan, and ten thousand men made up a tumen. This meant that each soldier lived within a small family unit with nine other soldiers, with no man higher than another. This expectation of equality meant that each man could prove himself based on his loyalty and military achievements rather than relying on his birth or name to progress through the ranks. A census was arranged so that every man would be counted and expected to fight. Armies could quickly be assembled from multiple tumens, creating large armies of as many as a hundred thousand soldiers. Armies this size, moving across the wide expanse of grassland with the families of the soldiers, their animals, and the supplies they would need, must have been an incredible sight to behold.

Psychological Warfare

Genghis Khan used psychological warfare to great effect, and this is partly why it is difficult for historians to get a realistic picture of the Mongol Empire. It is likely that stories of battles were greatly exaggerated in order to generate fear; Genghis preferred his enemies to submit willingly, and they were much more likely to do this if they believed that the Mongol forces were even more terrifying and merciless than they were.

Psychological tactics were also used in battle. These tactics included making the army look and sound larger than it was. Dummies would be placed on the backs of horses to give the impression of more riders, bonfires would be lit to make the nighttime camp look more extensive, and lots of noise was generated using drums. Demoralizing the enemy with shows of strength, silent attacks followed by deafening drum beats accompanying coordinated charges, and intimidating siege weaponry helped win the psychological battle before the Mongols had even engaged in battle.

Inclusion

One of the tactics that stands out the most when looking at Genghis Khan's military strategy is the policy of absorbing enemies into his own army. Subjugated enemies who submitted and were deemed worthy of inclusion in the Mongol army were spared death and joined the ranks of the army. Perhaps a mixture of gratitude, fear, and self-preservation transformed these one-time enemies into loyal soldiers, but perhaps the legendary charisma of Genghis himself and the quasi-religious fervor of his supporters converted those he had conquered.

The most compelling story of inclusion, and one that is often used to demonstrate the complex thought process of Genghis Khan, is that of Jebe. Jebe, originally named Jirqo'adai (Zurgadai in modern Mongolian), was an enemy soldier who fought against Genghis during his campaign to unify the tribes. During a battle, Genghis was wounded. After the battle was over, he asked his attendant to find out who had injured his horse (because it simply wouldn't do to admit that he himself was the target of the arrow). Zurgadai voluntarily confessed that it was he who had shot the arrow. His bravery and honesty impressed Genghis. Zurgadai went on to say that Genghis could kill him if he wanted, but if he spared his life, he would be a faithful and loyal servant. Genghis was so enthralled with Zurgadai that he renamed him Jebe, a Mongol name which means arrow, and gave him a position in his army. Jebe turned out to be a master military strategist, and he won many important campaigns for Genghis, whom he served faithfully as he had promised.

Chapter 6: Do Whatever Is Needed - Machiavellian lessons

This phase gets to the absolute core of Machiavellian thought and ideology. The entire is focused on the notion of doing absolutely anything that is necessary in order to achieve an intended objective. This concept, and nuances relating to it, will first be explored in the abstract before being updated for the modern world and applied to a number of different situations.

The absolute essential idea underpinning this concept is having a clear objective in mind at all times. It is not possible to exert influence in the Machiavellian sense without having a clear understanding of what you want to get out of any situation. People who exert control over others for their own sake are not Machiavellian. The true Machiavellian influencer always knows exactly what he or she wants to achieve at any given time and everything else is merely a way of getting what they want.

Have you ever heard the saying "the end justifies the mean?" If so, you are already familiar with a core pillar of the Machiavellian state of mind. Machiavelli taught that absolutely anything was justified if it served the aims of the influencer. Whatever it is you want to achieve in life, you should be willing to do absolutely anything needed to get where you want to go.

This is one of the Machiavellian ideas many people find difficult to grasp. Most people are trapped by conventional notions of ethics; thus, they struggle to grasp the concept of absolutely any course of action being fair game so long as it serves the aims of the person carrying it out. If you yourself subscribe to notions such as "fair play" and "playing by the rules" then you need to let these go in order to behave in a purely Machiavellian way.

What are the first steps to shed the concept of morality and ethics and behave according only to the notion of utility? The first understanding that must be reached is the idea that someone will inevitably be hurt no matter which course of action is pursued. Let's look at democracy, for example. Many people see this as an ethical and just system; however, in spite of its so-called "ethical" status, many people are hurt as a result of it.

Another example to illustrate this concept is the decision not to go to war. Though some may laud it as ethical, the result of this inaction is the likelihood that many people will suffer. If, for example, Iraq had not been invaded, how many people would have died at the hands of Saddam Hussein? This is yet another example of how behaving in an "ethical" way will still hurt people.

So, is Machiavelli saying that going against ethics will result in people not being harmed? Not in the least. Machiavelli instead stated that people would be hurt and harmed no matter which course of action a person pursues. Therefore, it is better to pursue a course of action that serves a broader aim. If people are to be harmed no matter what, surely it is better that they are harmed in pursuit of an aim, rather than harmed due to some mandatory, unexamined notion of ethics.

Another nuance of this concept that Machiavelli wished his readers to understand is that people will forgive absolutely anything if they benefit from it in the long run. This can be hard to grasp, but there are countless examples of how it is true. People may, abstractly, be against the notion of animal testing, but if such testing provides a cure, which benefits their own life, they will forgive the means by which that cure was discovered. As always, "the end justifies the means." This may be hard to grasp initially, but careful consideration will show it is almost always true.

The Update

There are many ways in which this concept is more relevant than ever in the modern world. We live in a society that constantly struggles with ethics and the right and wrong thing to do. Several illustrations will show how this concept is absolutely essential for the modern world to understand.

Let's take the example of torture; how many people living in a modern society, such as America, would say that they are okay with the notion of torture? A vast minority, probably; however, if there was a nuclear device planted somewhere in a major city, such as New York City, and the government had a suspect in custody who knew the location of the device, how many people would have a problem with the government using torture to find out the location of the device? Almost none.

Another facet of this idea, which must be updated for the modern world, is the notion of having an objective or aim. In the time of Machiavelli, the aims and objectives he talked about usually involved the conquest of kingdoms and the exertion of political power. The chance to conquer foreign lands is not one that many modern readers will have. This does not mean that the idea of having a clear objective and purpose becomes any less important. Let's further explore this idea of purpose in a modern light.

Modern society typically likes consumers to be as purposeless as possible. This is due to the fact that people without a clear objective can be easily influenced to serve the aims of others, such as corporations or political leaders. Having a clear objective and purpose is therefore a key component of being an impactful Machiavellian leader. There are various arenas though in which the notion of purpose becomes relevant, such as the corporate world. Some examples of a corporate, or professional, purpose include setting one's sights on the job held by another, influencing co-workers, or achieving a desired level of influence and control over others.

The financial world is another arena in which having a clear purpose can be helpful. If people have a distinct financial goal, such as making a certain amount of money by a certain period of time, then it lends their actions clarity and the goal is more likely to be pursued. Having a clear goal then allows people to apply the idea of "do whatever is necessary." For example, if someone needs a certain sum by a certain time, which is more important to him or her than ethics or the law, they may be willing to do whatever it takes to get it to be it theft, drug dealing, or anything unscrupulous. Modern readers need only to look towards the character of Walter White in Breaking Bad to grasp this notion; his purpose, to manufacture narcotics, was more important to him than his ethics—therefore he did whatever was needed to serve it.

The Application

In what ways can we apply this Machiavellian idea to our everyday world? The first key component is to have a clear objective or aim in any given situation. Also, it is important to think in terms of both macro and micro objectives. For example, a person may have the macro-objective of "make a lot of money." This may then translate down into smaller micro-objectives such as "exploit this person for X amount, steal X amount from this place," etc. The broader, macro aim or strategy is broken down into smaller, micro aims or tactics.

Whereas in Machiavelli's time, the notion of aim was likely to refer to a single, overarching purpose, such as "conquer this nation," the modern Machiavellian is likely to have a series of aims within different fields that coexist at the same time. For example, the modern Machiavellian may aim to "make this amount of money, get this person's job, sleep with this person," but all of these are aims that coexist and apply to different areas of life at once.

Once aims and objectives have been clearly defined and understood, the modern Machiavellian is able to always think in terms of "does this serve my aim?" A Machiavellian thinker needs to train their mind to the extent that thinking in this way is an automatic reaction at all times and any other forms of consideration whatsoever seem entirely alien and useless. Only by being utterly ruthless and dedicated in the pursuit of an aim is the modern Machiavellian able to serve it effectively.

The Machiavellian understanding that people will forgive anything as long as it serves them is also one that should be applied to as many aspects of modern life as possible.

The idea of "doing whatever it takes" is incredibly powerful when applied to the arena of personal aims, objectives, and goals. Often, it is the doubt of whether something can be achieved that holds people back from even attempting it. A firm understanding of "doing whatever it takes" is empowering in the sense that it makes people subscribe to the notion of "when there's a will, there's a way." If people are able to grasp the ideas of this phase fully, they will be able to find means by which to achieve their goals, no matter how big and ambitious the goals may be.

This idea has many uses within the world of business. For example, as a leader of a company, it may sometimes be necessary for people to lose their jobs. This may be painful for the individuals in question, but it is needed for the wider objective of the company surviving and being successful.

If the average CEO was to issue a survey to their workforce asking how they felt about the prospect of people losing their jobs, it is doubtful that many people would respond stating they were in favor of job losses. Most people would be vehemently against the idea and may even express outrage at it. On the other hand, if these same people had their own jobs saved as a result of others losing their jobs, how many do you think would have a real problem with it? How many people would volunteer to lose their own job to save that of another person?

Once you are able to internalize the notion of people forgiving almost anything if it serves them and you coincide this understanding with the power of having aims and objectives, you will experience a sense of great freedom and power.

Within the business world, you will be free to make the decisions that serve an aim and purpose that is greater than the given situation at the time. You will know at the deepest level of understanding that people will be hurt no matter what you do, so you should do what serves a greater aim. People will be hurt either way, but at least they will be hurt for a reason.

You will also be liberated from the concern of being a people pleaser. When you make decisions according to the principles of this, you will be able to free to have the knowledge that there is no such thing as "unforgivable" as long as people benefit in the long run. Your playbook's pages expand infinitely in number when you are free of the shackles of conventional morality and can instead act entirely freely, with single-minded focus.

Chapter 7: People Moralism - Machiavelli

How Man's Nature Changes

Machiavelli comments that men go from one state of mind to another. First, they seek security against aggression. Later, established as powerful men, they start offending others. While fearful, they seek release from fear; once powerful they spread fear in others. The very injury that they ward off in the beginning, they inflict on others later – almost as if it is a necessity to be aggrieved or to aggrieve others.

While in the first state of warding off attacks, men talk of virtues and kindness. The propaganda is primarily intended to serve as a protective shield. Once they are well inside the protective lap of security, now more powerful than others, they start attacking others. This is when they shed their moral overcoat.

Nowhere in Machiavelli's works is there mention of people who speak of, preach or practice virtue and kindness even after rising to power. Machiavelli perhaps does not believe that such people exist who would continue to be magnanimous, generous and kind even after acquiring power… Not only do they preach and speak about kindness but practice it even after rising to power. This means that the belief that 'power corrupts and absolute power corrupts absolutely' needs to be revisited. Whether power will corrupt or exalt depends more on the recipient. Power in Genghis Khan's hands could corrupt but Mother Teresa's hands might exalt.

In a nutshell, Machiavelli outlines the following growth chart from the benign to the malevolent.

First, a citizen just desires protection, seeks friendship; this he acquires through honest means or often even by bribing the powerful. Slowly he acquires power. The other citizens start fearing him and the powerful people start treating him with respect. Not only that, they start fearing him and his friends. Later, the magistracy (judges) also side with him. Such clout corrupts his thought and action and he turn completely selfish, often inhumane and evil. Such a man can be handled only through sudden ruin or extreme repression. So, you can either extinguish his evil with sudden action against him or await his death, while being servile to him during the period.

To avoid a potentially dangerous man becoming a monster, what must a person do? Bell such a cat today while it is still a stray on the streets. Once it grows into a vicious cheetah of the wild, you won't have that option.

On Taking Sides

In times of war, the one who is not your friend will wish you to remain neutral, while your friend will expect you to join his war. According to Machiavelli, when two people fight, you must surely take a stand in favor of one of them. A lily-livered Prince, to avoid risks and danger, follows the neutral path and is ruined.

How? Because when two of your powerful neighbors' fight and one of them wins, you will either fear him, or you won't. But if you have taken no stand, not made your loyalties known, you will fall prey to the ire of both. The winner will not be sure of your devotion, and now more powerful, might move to conquer you too. If you have fought in favor of the winner, he will never attack you on moral grounds. On the contrary, he will reward you. If, on the other hand, the other party you fought against wins the war, they too will understand and appreciate your level of loyalty and want you on their side. Another possibility would be your being sheltered by the loser and companions in a fortune that may rise again. According to Machiavelli, you cannot really avoid one trouble without running into another. Prudence lies in knowing how to read the character of troubles and to choose the wiser path.

Machiavelli, of course didn't have the benefit of seeing some nations e.g. Switzerland and even India which have survived and thrived despite their neutrality. This is because the nature of geopolitics has changed. Rather than going down one fixed path, countries go through phases. There are seasons for war, peace (or alliances) and for neutrality.

On Keeping Word

Of promises, Machiavelli said, a promise given was a necessity of the past; a broken word is a present necessity. In a style quite his own, Machiavelli advised, "Don't go by morals, and go by flexibility, go by utility; be a utilitarian."

Punishment Instead of Reward

Machiavelli pointed out that ingratitude was born out of jealousy or suspicion.

The example he used is one that has been witnessed again and again in history – of a victorious General returning home. The General had won the battle and his victory caused jealousy and insecurity in the Prince. As the General's power rendered his submission to the authority of the Prince needless, he is either executed or sidelined by the Prince.

Machiavelli pointed out that while doing this the Prince punished the one whom he should have rewarded, and he suspected the one whom he should have trusted. Machiavelli advised such Generals to either submit with humility to the Prince's authority, or take up arms against the Prince and grab power. He found the second course more honorable.

His advice to the Prince was to avoid being jealous or ungrateful. He advised the Prince to venture out in the battlefield for his own victories. And history is witness to the fact that many virtuous princes have done so by leading from the front.

Why One Must not Change his behavior suddenly

Machiavelli warns that during difficult times, favors should not be showered suddenly on those whose support you seek. If a war is on, or if an opposition flares up from outside the organization or from your superiors, think twice before obliging in a rush your juniors, for their support. Because, once they come to know the favors were due to your impending problems, they would also understand them to be temporary. Once out of your predicament, you might take them back. Once the problem is obvious to all, you will not only lose the required support, you could also accelerate your ruin for doling out favors at such times.

Machiavelli advises farsightedness to the Prince and to be aware of the hardships he could face. He must be prepared with a list of people who'll back him no matter what, on whose support he can fall back in times of need. He should wisely cultivate the friendship of such men before he gets into trouble.

As a corollary, Machiavelli says that whoever at one time feigns to be good, and then for selfish reasons wants to become bad, should do so gradually using proper means so that the change does not appear sudden or abrupt. This way, before his changed nature takes away old favors from him, he may get some new well-wishers so that his authority is not drastically reduced. If he changes suddenly from being humane to haughty, from being easily accessible to difficult to approach, his crude impropriety will leave him deserted and alone.

Why should you not Utter Threats or Use Harsh Words

Machiavelli advised people to avoid delivering verbal threats, for threats and insults do not dissipate the strength of the enemy. Instead, threats caution him, and insults lead to a more focused hatred and violent attack against you. It might very well induce the enemy to fire his most potent weapon onto you. Harsh statements leave a sting in human memory. Even if they are false, their harshness lingers.

Moreover, he says, be especially watchful against using dishonorable words against an enemy immediately after a victory or when you think victory is in sight. Victory or even a glimpse of a victory may make you arrogant and over-confident – both makings of – sudden failure. One should always guard against speaking harsh words at such junctures.

On How Good Actions Don't Heal Past Injuries

An old enemy of yours, whom you have hurt, will not become a friend just because you've changed your demeanor and are now showering him with favors. In desperate measures for damage control, the misery inflicting, victor-king has often tried to win over the victim-king with favors, but almost always in vain. As Machiavelli's experiences reveal, good actions can rarely write-off old injuries. So given a chance, the beneficiary would more likely avenge the wrongs done unto him than reciprocate the rights.

Be Good, Appear Good but be Capable of Evil as Well

A Prince should be good, yet if compelled, he should know how to be ruthless as well. While an appearance of a merciful, faithful, humane, upright and religious Prince is positive, his strength and power should be visible too.

Machiavelli insisted – appear good, but be well-armed too. According to him, the Prince controlled two different entities: one, the world outside his kingdom and two, his own people. He could defend himself from the external world by having a good arsenal and good allies. He was likely to have loyal friends and staunch allies if he was well armed. Being well-armed would also prevent internal rebellion and subordinates would think twice before challenging him.

Chapter 8: The Power Potential within You

Three emotional truth that could boost your inner power

A few of us will reach fantastic issues. The others won't. However, is this? All of us are only "chatting monkeys onto a natural space ship flying throughout the world," since Joe Rogan sets it. Therefore, why would a few "talking monkeys" assemble 8 or 7 figure organizations, traveling the earth, and are living the life span in their fantasies as the others folks... Appropriately, the desire we're living the life span of their imaginations.

What is the gap between these and us? The fantastic thing isn't just a complete lot. You're equally as competent because they're. You're equally as powerful and filled with possibility since they're. They only know that a couple of things concerning hacking on their psych and unlocking their internal power you most likely do not understand.

Here are three emotional details that may unleash your inner power:

1. Your ideas just determine the best way to believe

Through the majority of the 1900s, psychologists used behavioral treatment to successfully treat individuals who have anxiety, depressive disorders, eating problems, dependency, you identify it. All of us form of guessing, if you would like to adjust some body's activities, then you want to modify their activities!

It was around 1960 that Albert Ellis indicated the proven revolutionary fact concerning our profoundly held beliefs regarding the entire world (i.e., how we presume), precisely what he named our "fundamental snobby assumptions,' ascertain the way we believe and ergo, the way we act. It was subsequently implied that if you would like to alter your activities or behaviors, you need first to change the direction that you imagine.

Today, a whole division of psych, chased cognitive treatment, is specialized in this assumption. And that the consequences are somewhat shocking; drugs together with behavioral and cognitive therapy are currently 75 percent to 90 percent more effective. To put it differently, if you would like to improve how you act and the way you feel, then subsequently alter the direction that you believe. Much easier said previously, " I understand. Continue reading.

2. Your mind can not inform the gap between reality and imagination

Perhaps you have thought about something humorous that occurred after which captured your self-laughing or grinning at people? You've! Almost all of us have. However, is this? After all, the humorous issue happened -- therefore, why have you been talking about any of it at the moment? Properly, it is because the mind cannot tell the gap between reality and imagination.

In the event you envision a great thing occurring, then you'll encounter each of the beneficial emotions that you connect with this fantastic item as though it transpired. The same goes for unwanted encounters. That is this kind of revolutionary emotional actuality that one particular analysis demonstrated there isn't a lot of gap between picturing moving into the gymnasium and visiting the fitness center!

Therefore, how is this essential? It signifies that, using just a small amount of how intentionality, you can reposition the human brain to connect pleasure or pain with all these activities you pick. By picturing the near future consequences of one's lousy behaviors and also the long-term advantages of desirable behaviors, you're able to attest real enthusiasm to improve and also accept the very first faltering step in developing a new life which arouses you.

3. You are better in creating a brand fresh custom when you're currently ceasing a terrible routine

You can't ever give up a terrible routine, maybe you are not ready, at least. The custom pathway on your brain is formed, and there is no known solution just to infect that pathway entirely. However, you may transform the path. You may set a brand-new behavior within the habitual trigger-behavior-reward program. Charles Duhigg, " the author of the power of routine phone calls this "the golden principle of practice, adjust: "you cannot instill an unfortunate habit, so you may just change it out."

This is the reason why individuals who are making an effort to stop smoking, chew gum, and take alcoholics beverage caffeinated drinks -- as those things are substitutes to your terrible routine.

In a situation where you want to stop a particular habit such as overeating, oversleeping, smoking, drinking, etc. Don't make attempt to stop, consider starting something new to replace the old habit. Frequently, contemplating ending only leaves, you would like to participate together with the terrible addiction more as you are considering any of it! However, exchange the terrible dependence using something both gratifying, something fantastic for you, and you're going to have the ability to improve any unwanted behavior immediately.

How can you specify interior power?

Inner power could be your silent pressure within one who understands when to behave when to proceed and grants you the energy to achieve that.

Have you read about the story about a mother who lifted up an automobile with her bare hands to save her child that was trapped beneath? If that's the period of death or life, she tapped to her internal power. Someone could feel overly tried to walk or move; however, somebody should shout fire! He finds out the energy to perform.

This inner power is something most of us possess. However, we will need to master to tap it into imaginative and compelling methods within our day-to-day lifespan.

Now you climbed in the humblest of beginnings to accomplish expert power. What do you know concerning endurance?

To begin with, without having god, I'd not be right here now. What else would a small lady from the small village at Korea that was simply tagged a curse along with evil fortune grow up to turn into high-tech CEO, writer, motivational speaker, and much more?

Achieving my goals failed to arrive immediately. Step-by-step, I had to produce the requirements that could let me actualize my dreams.

To split from this box, individuals were attempting to help keep me trapped inside, " I needed to pick each day maybe not to permit hard predicaments to overpower me.

My first job when I came to the U.S was cleaning baths in a lodge. People called me a lot of dreadful names. I always needed to validate: "they're not my god. I was of who and exactly what I am. I understood exactly the way that led me there".

These struggles, " I heard an essential lesson: even though we could sense as though the barriers we confront are insurmountable, that is perhaps not correct. We have to continue to the fantasies and maintain performing our role as the upcoming massive breakthrough is waiting to input our own lives in only the most suitable minute.

Just as an urge for women's power, what you presume females most want to attain power?

On reach power, ladies want absolute and total honesty. When ladies might be frank and take their flaws in addition to their strengths, doorways of liberty and opportunity will probably open to them. Whenever you make up your mind and face a weakness, then you consistently benefit an increment of power as you're carrying the very first measure to grow.

Honesty also means, not exactly what someone expects you to become. Tapping into your internal power to remain faithful to a yourself can be the origin of everything I instruct: you're just one of some sorts. A daisy certainly not inquires itself, "why are not I personally an improved?" each portion of production, for example, you, has its beauty and also its strength

Precisely what may be the one most essential point to understand about every one of these methods above to interior power?

Even the seven measures to interior power are joining along the human entire body and mind as you can so that your thinking and activities are tasked accountable for one's own goals; detecting the facts yourself; attaining strength of human body-mind, and soul therefore that you may convey your authentic disposition; learning how to love yourself; preserving devotion for your targets and lifestyle; learning how to forfeit unnecessary and flaws pursuits and attachments therefore that you may accomplish your aims; and also trying patience at all that you need to do.

Even the most crucial point to learn concerning these ways above is which you simply can't perform you measure minus others should you genuinely want to split into fantastic. Every one of the steps come with each other to attract wholeness for your becoming.

Perhaps not every one of the hurdles people confront originates out of. What interior limits do persons, as well as maybe notably ladies, placed forth by themselves?

Most folks possess an interior conversation that states, "I am not adequate" or even "I really don't deserve it" or also "I don't have what it takes" this usually stems in several years of listening in to all other people's viewpoints folks overcritical moms and dads, covetous colleagues, aggressive allies, along with also others.

When we purchase inside that misinformation, we eventually become our own worst enemies. We usually do not cure ourselves nicely. If a person else handled you together with hate, criticism, or disrespect, then you'd not endure this. Therefore, what exactly makes it right that you treat yourself which manner?

Stop terrorizing yourself! It is the right time for you to alter your inner dialogue and understand and tune in and link up with your inner self (your authentic, initial self-explanatory and interior voice) that claims that you simply have all of the power you want to meet your fantasies.

All of us live in a civilized world where kids are taught to be afraid of making mistakes. Do you believe this is a smart path?

No! Once you make a mistake, then this indicates you're doing something. Is not this lovely? In the event you don't conduct anything, then you won't create errors, yet nevertheless, you won't receive outcomes, and you're going to go nowhere.

" I do not consider mistakes as something that is unwanted. I admit my response was not exactly what I required, therefore that I got to shift, explore longer, and also be much creative. I educate my pupils to study faults. Just as an issue of simple fact, I state: create an incredible blunder!

The best way many errors did alexander graham bell create when devising calling? Exactly how many blunders did engineers create even though acquiring the cell-phone? Who disagrees? The goal is always to triumph and not rely on your own mistakes. That is the reason my motto is "They could do, she could perform, you will want to me."

Chapter 9: Five Practices to Help You Be Your Best You

Deep down, you know that there is more you can be and do. The remorse you feel comes from knowing you could have handled a situation better than you did. You yell at your child over something small, and then you feel guilty about it for a day. You have a deadline for a project, but you procrastinate until you don't have a choice but to work all night long to get it done. You don't feel anything but anxiety the entire time you are doing it. This isn't anything new, humans have been putting things off that they have to do, obsessing over things they can't control, and giving into emotions for thousands of years.

There are certain times during the year that people get reflective. They begin thinking about the way the year began, where they are now, and the way they have or haven't changed. They reflect on things they could have done better, how they treated others, and what they didn't get done. Due to this, they make resolutions at the beginning of every year. They constantly say that beginning the next year, they are going to quit smoking, begin dieting, or start exercising more. But another year rolls around and then when they face difficulty, they cave and go back to their old ways.

They light a cigarette, start a fight with their partner, and constantly endure all their negative emotions that come when they disappoint themselves.

This isn't saying that keeping resolutions is easy. Changing habits never is, but this won't change the fact that this needs to be done. The Stoics knew all of this and they wrote about it to remind themselves to act virtuously. The point I'm trying to get across is that we have to be in a constant state of self-improvement, and there will always be an opportunity to practice this everywhere you go. You can waste those opportunities. Keeping this in mind, here are some practices that could help you in all walks of life, and it doesn't matter what your circumstances are or where you are from.

Practice the Things You Read

The reason most people study Stoic philosophy is to improve all facets of their lives. Stoicism is the most practical of all the philosophies. It doesn't worry about debating whether there is free will or complicated theories about the world. They help us get rid of our destructive emotions and act on the things that can be acted on. Its main purpose is to keep you calm when you are under pressure and focusing on your ideals to exclude everything else. There isn't any point in reading Seneca's letters if you aren't going to apply them immediately to your life. Marcus Aurelius knew that there aren't many things we have to do to become our best selves. These can be learned through theories but can't be completely absorbed through our experiences. You don't totally realize how powerful it can be to let go of your anger until you actually do it in a difficult situation. It will be amazing once you see how much peace you will feel when you do it. All of this is making you stronger and capable of handling future trials that you will be subjected to.

Books are there to keep you from bouncing all over the place. You won't be able to learn from your experiences, and you will be doomed to repeat these mistakes over and over again. They exist for you to refer back to when you need some counseling or anytime you need to remind yourself ways to deal with anger, and way to embrace hardships rather than getting emotional and making things worse.

Embrace Difficulties

The biggest downfall to our destinies is the way we react to the things that happen to us. Things don't cause it, we do. Think about who you admire; it is probably someone who has overcome difficulties and let it make them stronger and better. When anything bad happens, don't allow your first instinct to be to run from it. Allow it to be an opportunity to learn and to bring out your best. The more hardships you overcome, the stronger you will get. To quote Seneca: "There is no one more unfortunate than the man who has never been unfortunate. For it has never been in his power to try himself."

David Goggins once said: "The nice comfortable environment we are in right now makes us create lofty goals. What are you going to do when your New Year's resolution was to run every day, and when you wake up, look outside and see that it is snowing and it is negative two degrees?"

Everyone makes resolutions every year, and the main reason they aren't kept is that we give in to the easiest action when we face adversity. It is easy to make resolutions to not get mad easily when there isn't anything that is making you angry. The only thing that will make you better is when you keep promises that you have made to yourself. Hardships don't need to be some huge tragedy or event; everyone experiences small hardships daily. Will you let a traffic jam that took an extra hour ruin your day, or will you use this time to practice patience? These little events test us, but they also show us the tiny things that make up the fabric of our lives. If you constantly fly off the handle over every little thing, we aren't prepared to handle ourselves when something bad really happens.

You can take comfort in knowing that these tests that we go through daily are universal, and nobody can escape them. Marcus Aurelius had problems getting out of bed every day. He knew that nature has set limits on everything and that all hardships will eventually end. Maya Angelou said: "Every storm runs out of the rain." If you can tell yourself this enough, you might begin to see that all the hardships are making us appreciate the good times.

We are only able to reap the benefits if we practice this regularly by embracing instead of shirking from the hardships. When we do this, we allow ourselves to be grateful for the lessons that life teaches us, and for each moment.

Protecting Your Time

The worst thing about not keeping resolutions is you will regret it as the year goes by. You will eventually come to the end of your life and realize the time that you wasted. You will see how much you got in your own way. You will realize all the times you gave into anger when you had the power to avoid it. You will see how this impacted your life in a negative way.

When you make a commitment to practice Stoicism, you need to make sure that when your time is up, you are proud of all the things you did with the time that was given to you. When you make the best use of your time doesn't mean you have to keep busy all day long, it means that you have to make the best use of each moment as they go by. This means that you have to use every moment as a way to practice gratitude and presence. By doing this, you will get to the end of your life, knowing that you spent a very small amount of time being jaded or negative over the circumstances that life threw at you. You didn't spend your time scrolling through social media or giving in to your impulses. You spent it doing the work that you care about, making yourself better, and serving your community.

When you make the best use of your time, it means that you have to remember what you can control and act on things the best you can. It means that you leave nothing that has to be done undone. When you can do this, you will get to the end of your life being satisfied and not full of regrets, but you will be thankful for every opportunity that you used. To quote Marcus Aurelius: "Pass then through this little space of time conformably to nature, and end thy journey in content, just as an olive falls off when it is ripe, blessing nature who produced it, and thanking the tree on which it grew."

Acting Virtuously

The Stoics thought that the ability to become our best selves lies proportionately in how often we practice the four pillars of virtue: justice, temperance, courage, and wisdom. If you can make pursuing wisdom the main goal in your life, you can be sure that no matter what happens, you will be equipped to learn from all that happens to you. When you can practice courage, you will face every situation with strength and won't give up when things get hard. When you practice temperance, you will keep yourself from giving into excess and won't allow your emotions to get the better of you when it is important. When you can practice justice, you will know whatever outcome you get; you were trying to do the right things.

This isn't going to be east, and this isn't the point. The point is to practice the virtues every chance you get is the best way to improve yourself and to become your best self. Make a point to keep these virtues in the front of your mind whenever life gets a bit hard or your resolutions get tested.

Practicing Forgiveness

You are going to constantly be coming in contact with people who are going to test you. Marcus Aurelius knew this very well. He was always dealing with liars and charlatans. It wasn't easy for him not to want to get revenge. During these situations, he would remind himself that the best way to get revenge was "to not be like that." He knew he wouldn't ever be able to be his best self if he was always dwelling on the actions of other people. He knew that all he would get from allowing himself to give in to his anger was being reduced down to their level. He also knew that when he didn't practice forgiveness with others over the small things that didn't matter, he would make it harder to forgive himself when he made a mistake.

It is natural for humans to dwell on things when somebody did something bad to you or if we did something bad to ourselves. This keeps us from being able to move forward. If you can't forgive the people who wronged you, you will risk coloring all other relationships and interactions with those scars. If you can't forgive yourself, you aren't allowing yourself to move forward, and you won't ever be your best self. When you can forgive, you are letting go of your past, and you will be able to stop being a slave to it, and you will become your ideal self.

Chapter 10: Getting Started on Your 'Elite' Journey

Getting Started on Your 'Elite' Journey

The 'Elite' approach means changing your operations radically for the better – in order to become one of the 'Elite' in your business sector.

In my experience, you must have four things in place before you can make change happen successfully. These are:

- the rationale for making the change,

- a vision of what you are trying to achieve,

- a plan to take you from where you are to where you want to be, and

- the management capability to make it happen.

Let's look at each of these a little more closely.

Rationale

You must have a rationale or reason for making the change that you can express in one or two short sentences, and which everyone in the organization can understand.

Normally, the rationale has something to do with improving competitiveness, i.e., having to react to competitors taking your market share, or them selling at lower prices, or being more aggressive in the market place, all of which can impact your sales and profitability.

The rationale should always be genuine of course, but I have seen occasions when a client had a very strong market position but wanted to improve even further. To overcome a sense of complacency within the company, we actually created a pseudo competitive scenario to act as a rationale for the change program.

You will of course tailor the rationale to your particular organization and circumstances. Once you have it written and approved, you should then circulate it to everyone within the organization as part of your formal communications plan.

Vision

You'll form the vision of what you're trying to achieve from the work that you'll do as outlined in Module 2.

The three basic objectives that every 'Elite' program should have are to:
- minimize throughput time – to improve customer service, revenues and working capital,
- maximize throughput rate – to reduce internal costs and increase profits, and
- get it right first time – to help achieve the above two.

Your Practical Vision will incorporate targets for each of these three factors.

In addition, you will also establish what needs to happen in the key enablers that help you to achieve and sustain your Practical Vision. These key enablers are:
- synchronizing your main support functions, such as Quality, Engineering, IT, etc.,
- planning and scheduling, and
- organization.

Your 'Elite' Practical Vision, incorporating all of the above, will then form the basis of all of the analysis and implementation work that follows.

Plan

From Module 3 onwards I'll cover the details of how you develop a robust implementation plan that will help you to achieve your Practical Vision.

I have proved this highly structured plan in many hundreds of projects and it will give you the best chance of achieving success.

Management Capability

This is often the most difficult of the four elements.

If you're the leader of the business, then management capability will not be a problem – you will outline what needs to be done by whom and when, and provided you manage the program properly, you should get the results you want.

However, if you're not the leader of the business, it becomes more difficult. You need to have the endorsement of the business leader for the program, otherwise people will either pay lip service to it at best, or at worst will ignore it completely.

In the main, people do not want to change. They have an inbuilt reluctance to change the way they do things, and will only change when they see a logical or compelling reason for changing their behavior.

Someone once said that there are only three reasons why people change behavior – Love, Greed and Fear.

We can discard Love in this business context, so that leaves Greed and Fear.

Greed is not necessarily for more money. It could be greed for recognition or success in the eyes of colleagues or of competitors. Or it could be greed to realize a personal or business opportunity. Or it could be greed to enhance your personal status and get you into the best position for future promotion. Or it could be greed to increase your influence and authority within your business. Or it could be greed to improve the wealth of your business. Greed for success is a powerful driving force for changing behavior. It can get you into that virtuous circle of growth and success that all outstanding companies exhibit.

On the other hand, Fear is also a powerful driving force for changing behavior – fear of reducing job security or standard of living as competitors drive stronger and faster – fear of facing a business problem that you need to resolve – competitors being more aggressive – losing market share without really knowing why – costs increasing too much – profits falling steadily year on year – having difficulty attracting the best people – slowly getting into a vicious circle of decline.

So, in developing the management capability to make change happen successfully, you need to use Greed and Fear in a balanced way. Too much of either is a bad thing and will switch people off. Too little and there will be no incentive to change. You just need to think carefully about how you use these two factors in your situation, and I'll give you some helpful techniques to do this in Module 4.

Once you understand that these four elements need to be in place, you can then start your 'Elite' journey.

You need to consider:
- the process you're going to improve as a pilot,

- the members of the core project team, and
- your communications.

Let's look at each of these separately.

Process

Firstly, you need to sort out which process you're going to improve as a pilot project.

You should select the process that currently gives you the biggest headaches in terms of customer service, reliability or costs, or which takes too long or has too much rework.

You should also use the full end-to-end process for the pilot. Too many other practitioners will try to encourage you to take an initial relatively simple approach of focusing on individual elements of the process, but this misses out on the potential benefits that you can gain from considering the end-to-end process as a whole.

In general, I recommend that you start with a pilot project where you can learn how to create an 'Elite' solution and achieve radical objectives for Thruput Time, Thruput Rate and Right First Time that will deliver significant operational, financial and business benefits. You can then roll out similar solutions quickly to other products or processes.

The alternative of a 'big bang' approach, where you look at several products or processes at the same time, usually just makes the initial project way too complicated, and will more likely lead to failure.

Hot Insider Tip

A few years ago, I was asked to go into a company in the US to apply my 'Elite' approach. It turned out that they had already used a leading US firm of consultants to train their people and to start them on the process of applying Lean in their plant.

However, the consultant involved had given up after a couple of days at the plant and gone home because he said the application was too complex for Lean. The guys in the plant struggled on trying to make sense of it – but to no avail.

I didn't know this at the time of course and came in with my more advanced 'Elite' approach and applied it successfully from the start. We achieved fantastic results that helped to transform the business. Productivity increased by over 30% and manufacturing lead times reduced by over 75%, resulting in inventory savings of over $40 million.

One of the team members told me much later that their previous consultant had struggled for two days and then given up over something that I had resolved in less than five minutes.

Apparently, he had a problem in choosing the right product for the pilot program because there were lots of different products within this complex company. However, I simply took a product that had the biggest volume and which passed through most of the key manufacturing operations. It took just a few minutes to decide.

And that's all you need to do. Don't get hung up on the detail. Just sort out the biggest volume product – and take the biggest volume variant of that product – and make sure that it goes through most of the manufacturing operations. Just go for it.

Manufacturing Processes

In a manufacturing process, you should identify the product that you will follow for your pilot project. As in the Hot Insider Tip above, this product should be one of your biggest volume products that passes through most of the key production operations.

You also need to define the scope of the end-to-end process up front, particularly the start and end point.

Usually, in a manufacturing process, the start point is when the base raw material arrives at the unloading dock, and the end point is when the finished products leave the loading dock.

So, for example, in a furniture manufacturer, the start point would be when the base wood arrives at the site. The process would then follow the wood as it converts into a desk, where it goes through cutting, shaping and smoothing, then to assembly where the legs are put on, then through final sanding, finishing and packing until the finished desk is ready to ship at the loading dock.

In a pharmaceutical manufacturer for example, the start point would be when the active ingredient arrives at the site and the end point when the finished pack of tablets is in a box and palletized ready for shipping.

Hot Insider Tip

You should initially only consider a process within a site. However, occasionally you may face two very different processes on the same site where one feeds the other. In these circumstances, it makes sense to develop the 'Elite' Practical Visions separately, then bring them together later to get the full end-to-end process.

For example, the pharmaceutical company may have a separate chemical process on site making the active ingredient. This chemical process would be a very different process from the one making the final pharmaceutical product and it would therefore make sense in this instance, to keep them separate initially, then bring them together once you have the ideal Practical Vision for each.

The same would apply if the two different processes were on different sites. First, develop the Practical Vision for each process, then bring them together to get the combined process and the full end-to-end 'Elite' Practical Vision.

In one instance some years ago, we linked two sites across the Atlantic, and developed a trans-Atlantic kanban system to manage the link and give us a fast and highly efficient international end-to-end process.

Chapter 11: The Laying of Plans, Calculation and Estimation - Sun Tzu and Machiavelli

In the business world, it is very important to make plans that will continually act as a blueprint for your business. Earlier I talked about the importance of having

A strategy and how it matters to your business. You do not want to be left without a plan for your business as a business owner or as the leader of a team in whatever industry your business might be in. In order for a business to be successful in today's world of business marked by its unique features, it is very important that you have a blueprint that will act as a map towards the direction where the business is going.

As a popular saying goes "those who fail to plan already have a plan to fail". The truth is that

There is hardly any business that became successful by luck, for a business to become "lucky" in the first place, and then such a business must have made necessary plans or taken necessary steps beforehand. Why is it important for you to lay plans for your business? Why is it important to have the future in sight and operate based on what you look forward to becoming? If you want your company to become a multi-million dollar or possibly a multi-billion-dollar company then you must be willing to make plans to that effect. One thing I always love to tell business owners is that the period where it seems like a business is at the peak of its affairs is the period that such a business needs to work the hardest. You cannot get to the top of your market and choose to relax, that is basically what I call "business suicide". The business world is war, every single day when your business seems to experience growth, there is a very high possibility that a similar business is planning to take over from you. Therefore, it is not enough for you to make plans on how to get to the top of the list in your market, it is more important that you plan on how to remain there. When you take out time to properly plan your business, it is Quite obvious. Not only does this increase productivity amongst the members of your team, it also boosts everyone's confidence and definitely impresses your clients. The success of a business just like having victory on the battlefield is a result of proper planning. No successful company becomes successful by accident; it is as a result of adequate planning. I am a huge sports fan and one thing that I have come to cherish about sports is the fact that it shows you the unparalleled importance of planning ahead. If you plan ahead, you will be able to predict the future and there is a huge chance that you will have the solution to any problems that will arise later on.

Stay prepared   In Life, change is a constant thing and in the world of business, staying relevant is not as easy as it seems. Circumstances are bound to change and unforeseen events can change the fate of a business. I always emphasize the need to stay prepared for the worst-case scenarios in business, although that advice may seem somewhat pessimistic but it is the reality that people face in the world of business. The truth of the matter is that no one can perfectly predict what will happen in the future, you can at best make informed predictions. In order for you not to be caught unawares, it is important for you to always stay prepared, stay ready so you do not have to get ready when the storm comes. While we cannot predict the future, we can decide to adequately plan and prepare for it. By staying prepared, you are more likely to have a better response when the storm comes because you have always stayed ready. How then can you stay prepared in the business world? As much as we desire control and predictability for our business, the sad reality is that uncertainty is a part of business. I love classic stories about war because they tell you how important it is to always prepare and make plans for the future. In the business world, several companies and businesses have lost their relevance within the twinkling of an eye. The fact remains that nothing is guaranteed and the relevance of your business tomorrow is not guaranteed. Therefore, the best decision that you can make is to ensure that you prepare yourself and your business for the future the best way possible.

Finding your enemies

One of the most difficult things to do (mostly for the people who are less observant) is to recognize an enemy. They are in every aspect of our lives and most

Times, they even disguise as our biggest fans because they would rather avoid suspicion. I said it earlier that the business world is a battlefield and this makes it necessary for you to; prepare adequately, recognize the enemy and finally Strike. In any war, you are bound to have allies as well as enemies therefore it is important that after you must have prepared adequately then you should recognize who your enemies are. Unlike in the world of everyday human interactions, enemies in the world of business aren't always as a result of personal differences or because they hate you. Most times enemies in the business word are just people that wish for their business to succeed (at the expense of yours). The earlier you fish these enemies out then the quicker you can set them aside and burn them. I always urge business owners and leaders to embrace the idea of having an enemy. Having an enemy means that there is someone who would rather have the great thing you desire for you and your business and most times this comes at your own expense. This mere fact should act as a motivating factor for you to get to the next level.

There are various kinds of enemies in the business world. There are certain enemies who disguise as friends and these are the worst types of enemies to deal with. They act friendly with you in order to earn your trust and once you let your guard down, they strike you badly. One way to avoid falling into this trap is by not trusting anyone because by putting your trust in people, you are slowly digging your own grave. What I have come to notice over time that most times the biggest enemies we face are not other people but internal enemies such as fear, impatience, greed, laziness amongst others. Earlier I listed patience as an attribute of great leaders, patience will help you to notice certain character in People and this will ultimately help you to find your enemies and that is one major aspect in dealing with them. Once you are able to recognize who you enemy is then you should take out time to observe such a person/groups of persons and figure out the behavior of such person/set of people because by doing that will be understand their weak points and that is how you will strike them down.

Importance of planning is one of the most important aspects of running a business; it could be a large company planning its expansion or a small ne trying to gain relevance in its industry. The size of a business does not matter when it comes to planning; it is something that every business that wants to be successful must do in order to attain that success that they desire. Often times, I love to cite the example of a person going on a holiday trip; for that kind of trip, you are going to make certain arrangements as regards where you'd stay during the trip and so on(except you are one hell of an adventurous person). In the same vein, it is very important to plan in a business because not only does it give you a roadmap towards the end that you desire, it also makes the journey a lot easier as you are bound to make certain preparations for the months and years ahead. For a small business owner, you might not really see the point of planning (especially if you are the only one in the business at that time). In order for you to be able to successfully set your business strategy, you are going to need a business plan. Every business that exists is there for a reason or a set of reasons, there are certain goals, certain yardsticks for success, and certain needs that the business looks to meet and so on. Therefore, setting off a business without adequate planning is like testing the depth of a water body with both feet (which you will agree that is not very wise to do).

There are several benefits that come from having a business plan and I will concisely mention a few of them;

- A business plan will give you an honest assessment of your business' strengths and weaknesses (through the SWOT analysis).
- A business plan also helps you to properly state and explaining the strategies that you want to use when it comes to marketing.
- Also, having a business plan can be helpful with regard to getting the real value of your business. The plan will help you to understand how much your business is worth.
- Investors always require a business plan before putting their resources into the business.

There are several other benefits of a business plan that I would rather not bore you with. The whole point of this is to understand that it is necessary to make plans for the future of the business. The economy is not always very predictable and it can always spring up surprises therefore I urge you to always make plans looking forward and ensure that you follow these plans to the letter for the success of your business.

Chapter 12: The Principles of Time Management - Sun Tzu and Machiavelli

Sun Tzu argued that "most of us spend too much time on what is urgent and not enough time on what is important". When people learn about time management, they end up concluding that it is all about keeping yourself busy. While this is far from the truth, it is quite unfortunate that most people get confused about maintaining a busy schedule. There are instances where a busy schedule might deter you from gaining anything meaningful from your life. You will always be blinded from realizing this due to the perception that you are accomplishing something. In a real sense, you are robbing yourself of precious time. You need to wake up and distinguish between being productive and being busy.

Success in your life will depend on where your focus lies. This means that you ought to pay attention to priorities above anything else. What is important in your life right now? As you go through your daily life, what are those things that you classify as essential? These are your priorities and your efforts should be toward making them your primary tasks.

Determining Your Priorities

There are numerous activities that you will want to take part in during the day. However, it is worth realizing that not all these tasks are important. Most people struggle to distinguish between important and unimportant tasks. Usually, this is what influences the decisions that they end up making because they find themselves wasting time on unimportant assignments. So, how do you define your priorities?

Your priorities can be determined by knowing your values, goals, responsibilities and the effects of the activities that you engage in.

Defining Your Values

Following what has been about time management, it is now clear that by managing your time, you will also be managing your life. However, it is also important to clarify that you will not manage time effectively if you lack the motivation to do so. This fact makes it important to define your values. Your main reasons for trying to use time wisely should be attuned to something that you regard highly. Where do you find your motivation to wake up in the morning and go to work? People are different and therefore they all have varying motivations for setting goals.

So, before thinking of finding ideal strategies to manage time, start by defining your motivation. Good time management ought to be in harmony with your values. These two cannot be separated. Get it clear that if your efforts to take control of how you use time are not in line with your values, you will not be self-driven toward your goals and ambitions. Therefore, your first step toward effective time management should be to ask yourself the question, why? Why are you doing this in the first place? What is the main reason behind your efforts to try and control how you use time?

Find Your True Purpose

According to Buddha's teachings, the main purpose that you have in your life is to find your purpose ("Purpose Quotes," 2019). Accordingly, you should put your mind, soul, and heart into the process of unveiling your true purpose in life. This is the best way to move beyond living your life full of regrets and disappointments. Normally, most people go through their lives feeling frustrated because what they are doing is not meaningful to their lives. In other words, if they had the option of doing something else, they would quickly do it.

Time management defines your life in profound ways. But before that, you should have the right reasons behind your need to control time. In this regard, it would not be helpful to manage time when you know that whatever you are doing adds little or no value to your life. The point that we are trying to drive home here is that your time management purpose ought to be something that you love or something that defines your true purpose in life.

What Are Your Values?

The actions that you take toward successful time management should be in line with your core values. This is the only way through which you will garner the fulfillment you are looking for by changing how you utilize time. You have often heard business experts argue that for you to succeed in your business, you have to love what you are doing. This is what Richard Branson, founder of the Virgin Group, tells entrepreneurs (Gibbs & Fujita, 2019). A passion for what you do will help you realize that you are not just working for the money. You will see the bigger picture of running a business that is changing the lives of people in the community.

We all know a friend who earns good pay and yet is always complaining about his job. So, it is never about money. If your job is that important to you, chances are that you will care less about how much you are earning. Equally, you will not go through the frequent burnouts that we see most employees and employers going through.

When your life is defined by what you value most, there is an endless flow of energy within you. People around you will always wonder why you never get tired doing what you're doing. Therefore, it is very important that you spend time examining what your core values are. This should be followed by your efforts to try and make changes in your life which will guarantee that your actions and core values are in harmony.

Knowing Your Responsibilities

Your responsibilities will also have a role to play in determining your priorities. The responsibility of an employee, for example, is to work and join forces with other workers in a company. Folks with families also bear the responsibility of providing for their families. Bearing this in mind, the responsibilities that you have in your life will have a profound effect on your priorities.

Strategies to Help You Prioritize Your Most Essential Goals

Maybe you have been beating yourself up over the idea that you can't make the most out of the little time that you have. Well, cut yourself some slack because you are not alone. Most people struggle to use their time wisely and still find additional time to engage in other activities. The following strategies should help you utilize your time in the best way possible.

Designate a No-Work Time

Undeniably, we all have varying perceptions of how we prioritize activities at home and at work. It is interesting to know that there are some notable CEOs who manage to spend time enjoying their families. Susan Wojcicki, YouTube's CEO, fits into this category. In spite of her busy schedule, she still finds a way to spend meaningful time with her children (Ault, 2019).

There is an important lesson that you can learn from YouTube's CEO: You cannot be busy all the time. It is crucial that you spare some time where you don't work. The benefit of doing this is that it gives you an opportunity to renew your energy for work. Likewise, engaging in activities that are not related to your work helps to boost your creativity. Prioritizing doesn't necessarily mean that you should only schedule tasks that are work-related. Your mind also needs time to relax. This period is equally as important as prioritizing what you value as important in your working routine.

Planning Beforehand

Creating a to-do list is an ideal way of making sure that you are on top of the game with regard to time management. A common problem that most people face is forgetting to add important tasks to their lists. To evade this problem, the best thing to do is to create your list in the evening. During this period, you have ample time to think about what you will be doing the following day. In the morning, you are usually in a hurry and it is quite likely that you will forget to include important assignments and meetings in your to-do list. So, planning the next day in the evening can help a lot as you will wake up knowing how your day will progress.

Schedule Important Tasks

Another great idea that you can incorporate when prioritizing essential tasks is to schedule them. Find some spare time when you are most active and handle the tasks that you consider most important. Doing this relieves you of the pressure that you would have faced if you failed to complete these tasks. Moreover, you will work efficiently when your mind is relaxed.

Take Control of Your Time Usage

The amusing thing about time management is that you have the power to take charge of what you do. It all depends on the choices that you make. You can choose to spend your productive time doing unproductive work like going through your social media pages. Alternatively, you also have the power to mute your notifications and focus on your work for a particular period.

To effectively prioritize what you do, it is vital that you comprehend that you need to take control of your time usage. It is your responsibility to make informed choices which will guarantee that you spend your time productively.

Chapter 13: Maintaining Dominance

Dominance is not something you just earn and then keep for the rest of your life. It is something you must repeatedly work to maintain. Other people will vie for your position of dominance, so you can easily lose your throne if you are not careful. You must maintain dominance and make sure no one else takes it from you. Basically, you will be fighting for your entire life to maintain your dominance. Trust me, others will try to take it! It is not a nice world and no one will be content letting you have all of the power. You will always make enemies and run into opponents in life.

But do not let that overwhelm you. You will do fine. Here are some tips on how to maintain dominance that will be foolproof and relatively easy.

Always Be Alpha

To be dominant, you must always maintain your alpha status. Always wear that mask and project your dominance in all situations, even if you feel intimidated. Do not let anyone ever see you weak, down, or full of doubt. If you maintain this alpha status, people will never think to challenge you or doubt you. You will continue to earn respect and maintain dominance everywhere, every time, with everyone.

Two Methods

There are two methods to maintain dominance: by ensuring your submissive subject never gains power over you and threaten him with ruin if he rebels against you; or by convincing the submissive that the situation is not so bad and it is better to submit to you than to not.

The first is similar to the tactic that dictators use. You use fear to coerce someone into submitting to you. You can see that it is an effective method, but it eventually fails as people become angry and rebel against the dictator, bringing him down from his throne. Keep in mind that threats only work so far before they start to fail.

On the other hand, if you make people want to submit to you by making them love you or showing them the benefit of submitting to your will, you earn more fans and lasting loyalty. Convincing people to love you and submit to you is ideal because it makes people choose to submit to you. This eliminates the risk of rebellion later.

Which method you choose to employ for dominance is up to you and it depends on the situation. But you must choose a method. Once you gain dominance, you are permanently fighting for it. You are struggling to maintain. You must maintain dominance to remain successful or all your hard work is lost forever.

It is a lot harder to regain something you have lost because you prove that you are incompetent and lose respect when you let your dominance slip. Instead, keep it and it will be easier to maintain over time as you get into the habits of being a permanently dominant person and an alpha at heart.

Make Someone Be Your Friend

Being someone's friend is a great way to get their cooperation and submission. You also make sure that the person does not attempt to rebel against you or bring you down out of hatred. You spend time building affection rather than anger and resentment, making your subject love you enough to actually enjoy submitting to you. The power of influence also increases with friendship, as per the liking principle, where a person is more likely to do something for someone that he or she likes.

So, if you want to become a leader, you must also become someone's friend. But hang on. You want to differentiate between friendship where both friends are equal comrades, and the type of friendship where you have dominance. You must maintain your dominance with these "friends." Otherwise, they will feel too comfortable with you and will attempt to take advantage of you.

The best thing to do is to be the dominant, bossy friend from the start. Or you can be ruthless and gain dominance using tips highlighted above, and then later go about treating your subjects more like friends. Either way, be sure to maintain some dominance in the friendship. Sure, you can smile, chat, and laugh. But you still get to say what is up and make the decisions. You also get to drop your happy face and take some disciplinary action as necessary to get your subjects to mind your orders.

When you notice that your subjects are starting to lose respect for your authority or struggle with you for power, you need to assert your dominance all over again. Be sure to do it sooner than later to prevent too much damage to your dominant reputation. Start to get aggressive to show your friends what you are made of. Get surly and angry and demand respect. Or act insulted and hurt that they are violating the terms of your friendship by disrespecting your boundaries. As a co-worker or boss, this tactic is especially useful because you have the excuse that you are doing your job to make people feel better about it when you need to regain dominance.

Being moody and switching from friend to boss is a great way to maintain dominance without becoming a dictator. This roller coaster keeps people from getting complacent. It shows them that you are not just a buddy, but rather the one in charge. In addition, people start to stay on their toes, worrying about what you think and trying to keep you in friendly mode. So, start by being a very friendly, relaxed, and pleasant person to be around. But then switch to a hard, emotionless face when you give orders. Don't let your friendliness interfere with your boss mode. Never feel like you cannot take charge over those who are under your dominant wing.

As a leader, be open to others. Hear their ideas and use their input as you make a decision. The decision is still yours to make and you can decide whatever you want. But lending your subjects an ear makes them feel validated.

Positive reinforcement also works wonders over being a dominant jerk. Instead of criticizing people, tell them what they do well and reward or congratulate them on jobs well done. Show them lots of gratitude when they do what you want. Make them feel like you are all on a team by using "we" terms a lot and congratulating them on being excellent team members or helping you out. However, be sure to maintain your dominant status by giving everyone guidance, telling people no sometimes, and thanking them in a manner that makes it seem that they are not indispensable and are not somehow above you now or in your debt. For example, say things like, "Thanks for doing that so well" instead of "Thanks for doing that for me! I owe you one!"

As a leader, you can get involved in your subject's personal life. Asking personal questions and showing an interest may seem flattering to your subject. But in reality, it is giving you a ton of control and power. The more involved you get, the more power you get. So, try to get involved and seem like a friend about it. Meanwhile, offer advice and start to become more and more controlling. The subject will not realize what you are doing since you appear to be coming from a place of friendliness and helpfulness. And you get control over that person's personal life. This is especially easy and simple when you are already personally friends with someone.

At work, you can be a friendly boss. The important thing is to be less involved personally and emotionally. Hanging out after work is probably a bad idea, for example. Getting too personal can corrode the boundaries that need to exist for you to be a professional boss. Your friends can start to resent you for asking them to do things and they may think that they can get special favors from you or exist above the rules at work. Offer smiles and laughter all that you want, but definitely never drop the mask you wear as a boss. Be sure to always give orders and be above everyone. Make people like you so that they are more likely to do what you want and to minimize spite. But don't let yourself like them back.

Be the Dictator

If you choose to go the other route, of using fear to get people to hold you in high regard, then you must be the type of person to strike fear in your subjects. Otherwise, your plan will not work. Be prepared for people to talk crap about you and to resent you and resist you as much as possible. Being ruthless and putting an immediate end to any and all grumbling.

Your subject is absolutely at your mercy. This means that you must make your subject miserable. Show him or her what harm and pain you are capable of inflicting. This way, he will do what you want in order to avoid the harm and pain you can wreak upon his life. Showing your subject your bad side now and then is a good way to remind him of your power so that he will remain submissive.

The best thing to do is to have dirt on someone. Knowing something about him or her that will ruin him or her. He or she will be submissive and will do what you want to avoid getting in trouble with you. Use anything you can as blackmail to hold over someone. Maybe you can threaten to fire someone if he keeps avoiding certain tasks, or threaten to expose something you know about him to his wife. Or you can use simple emotional blackmail, where you make someone feel awful about himself and so guilty for being a horrible person that he will do anything to try to get you to see him in a more positive light.

Now and then, make an example out of someone to prove to your subjects what will happen if they go against your will. Get brutal and absolutely hurt someone to the core emotionally. Make sure someone loses something that he or she loves. This shows how powerful and ruthless you are.

Micromanagement is also key. Have something to say about everything. Give lots of orders and set lots of rules. This way you are injecting your dominance into every situation. Your presence is always noticed and felt. You never let your crown slip off your head because you are always dictating, always the boss of every situation. People have to ask for your permission and independence is punished, as well. You don't want free thinkers or independent workers. Everyone must turn to you for permission to do anything.

The important thing is to never be a good person. Be a scary person. Never let your guard down or show your heart. This makes someone fear you and hate you. He will do anything to avoid your wrath.

Chapter 14: The Principle of Success & Happiness in Business & Life

Principle 1: Most aspects of business and life involve never ending psychological battle.

You are reading the words of a complete schmuck, so take everything I say with a grain of salt.

Wouldn't it be nice if all authors admitted what I just said? The world would surely be a lot less confusing if they did.

You are wise to be reading this guide, but you are also wise to be skeptical about what I say... But please keep an open mind. I will walk you through the sobering realities of business and life, but I will not leave you without hope, faith, and a plan of action for success and inner-peace.

This phase is about the private struggles we all go through.

No one likes to talk about them. Most of the times we can't even put our finger on what's really happening as we're going through them. But the truth is that we are constantly in psychological battle.

A coworker says something. A friend does something. A client closes their account with you. A family member asks you for something. A vendor refuses to fulfill their promise to you.

When these things happen, we think about they we want. We think about what we want. We try to understand our own mind and understand theirs. And our moments of reflection and response cost us valuable time and energy.

Moreover, we construct visions of what we want on our own and then go out into the world to pursue them. Inevitably, other people's desires come up against our own. There is conflict. There is battle. And that battle is often purely psychological.

Not everything in business and life is adversarial, but much of it is.

The world we live in is transforming rapidly. In a world of constant transition, there is uncertainty. When there is uncertainty, there is aggression. And because the world is transitioning at an increasingly accelerated pace, it will only become more and more aggressive. You must face reality and prepare yourself for never-ending psychological war.

You may think I'm being overly dramatic or cynical. Fine. Be that way. I don't expect you to necessarily agree with me. What I respectfully ask of you, again, is to keep an open mind. This guide is about the way the world really works and what you can do about it. These principles, when understood and implemented with wise combination, will make you the best psychological warrior you can be.

Your time, energy, talent, and mental strength are your currency in psychological warfare. Resources such as money just posture you better, but they don't necessarily protect you.

Battles lie within battles. Wars lie within wars. And in today's world you must carefully choose your battles. But it isn't easy. Others will tempt you, bait you, and seduce you into conflict.

Most battles are psychological and psychological warfare is unavoidable and endless. To keep your sanity, you must work to understand and ultimately master the psychological warfare of everyday life.

Principle 2: Self-interest rules the world.

Want to know why the world is so screwed up? Self-interest. The world you inherited was screwed up. The world you may leave your children will be screwed up. Why? Because human beings are fundamentally driven by self-interest. I'm not saying that you can't do good things in the world or that certain areas of life aren't improving, but people's self-interest will come at you virtually every second in a myriad of ways. And many times, their self-interest conflicts with your self-interest.

It's okay for you to have self-interest and it's okay for the other 7 billion people in the world to have self-interest. There is nothing inherently wrong with this. It just means that battle is never-ending. Want to know when war as we know it will end? When there are no people left on the planet.

Sometimes people hide behind organizations or corporations. But behind these fronts are usually one or two key decision makers and they are the ones waging war on you, not the corporations they hide behind. Moreover, sometimes the self-interest of a person may slightly conflict with the interest of the organization that they hide behind, and if you are strategic, then you may be able to get that person to back down by exploiting this gap.

For now, understand that self-interest rules the world and that it is the reason you are constantly being kicked around in business and life.

Principle 3: The personal paradox: everything is personal, yet nothing is personal.

Bear with me here. This is a bit of a tricky and deep concept, but nonetheless, it's an important one to articulate at this point in our dialogue. Business life and personal life are emotionally inseparable. And when people come at you, it's very hard not to take it personally.

The thing to understand is that people pursue their self-interest. They may say things that appear personal, but this is just a tactic to demoralize you so that their self-interest can be advanced. In this sense, people make things personal, but it is purely rooted in the pursuit of their self-interest.

When people come at you in life, they are objectifying you. They are literally treating you like an object. Thus, there is nothing to take personally. The master warrior constantly works on and refines his personal psychology so that the actions of others don't cause him to self-destruct as a result of taking attacks personally.

Not taking things personally is easier said than done. I will address aspects of this problem later in this guide. For now, understand that it is to your advantage not to take attacks from others personally and to assume you are merely being objectified by the opponent.

Principle 4: You cannot avoid attack. The world will exploit you.

If you think you can avoid the world of psychological warfare, you are sadly mistaken. You can be in denial, but you cannot be in peace, for the self-interest of others will inevitably cause them to come after what you have. There are tactics which can deter others from coming after you, but aggression from opponents cannot be completely demolished.

People pursue their self-interest and will take everything from you that they can. Don't think that you can hide somewhere and avoid this. For instance, if you tried to hide from life by being a hermit in the woods, some other hermit would come along and try to take your cabin. So, don't even fantasize about avoiding attack, you silly hermit.

Principle 5: If all is fair in love and war, then the concept of fairness has little to no value.

Forget about fairness. Nothing in business or life is fair. There will likely be no justice for you when you are attacked or exploited. Typically, the most practical reason to play the "fairness" card is as a tactic to shame the opponent, and only if it can help position your self-interest.

When you feel like you've been treated unfairly, it's possible that the law or some other governing rules may protect you, but in most cases, there is nothing you can do about it except to refine your skills for future battles. Channel your feelings of injustice into strengthening your warrior skills and you will be making the most of your situation.

Principle 6: Choose your battles carefully.

In life you have a very finite amount of time and energy; psychological war will severely drain you of these precious resources. Just because you are attacked doesn't mean you have to attack back. You do not have the strength to fight every war.

Do not wage psychological war with others just because you can, for that is a waste of energy. Take a deep breath, step back, and carefully think through the cost of going to war and whether the probabilistic payoff is worth the cost.

You cannot avoid the attack, but you don't have to engage every opponent. Indeed, most opponents are not worth waging war with. Ask yourself, is the payoff worth it? Is this war worth it? Will fighting this opponent make something of me?

Remember, your time and energy are your most precious resources in life. Use them wisely.

Principle 7: It is better to die by the sword when you live by the sword.

Fine, I'm being dramatic again. But there is timeless truth in the adage that this principle is based upon.

Yes, "if you live by the sword, you may die by the sword" but you'll probably die by the sword anyway, so why not get a sword and learn how to use it so that you can live a little better?

The trick here is to attack the right people. Attack the opponents who stand in your way and who you believe you can defeat or gain an advantage from.

Embrace the sword and judiciously choose your battles, for this is the only rational way to live.

Principle 8: People are magnificent actors on the stages of business and life; judge them based on their actions, not their words and presentations.

Many people in the world live in self-deceit. This is dangerous because they truly believe they are being sincere when they articulate their supposed good intentions and lack of self-interest. You must be on guard when this happens.

I'm not saying that you should not trust anyone. Nor am I suggesting that you succumb to paranoia. But I am saying that you should remain vigilant and analytical. You see, there is such a thing as healthy skepticism. And the best acting talent is not on television or the cinema, it's in the people who come after you.

So, judge people by what they do, not what they say.

Furthermore, I challenge you to become a master psychological warrior in life; I challenge you to look deeply into yourself. There is perhaps no greater gift I could give to you but this challenge. I believe you are up for this challenge by virtue of you having read to this point. Do you believe you're up for this challenge?

Please believe in yourself. You must keep the faith.

Chapter 15: Psychological Strategies to give you an Advantage in Life

Manipulation, persuasion, and deception are the key trios in dark psychology, but they do not cover all the skills you need to be successful. The following tips and hacks will allow you to enjoy your environment with confidence. Knowing how to survive certain situations will give you the upper hand and who doesn't want that?

Interesting facts from day-to-day life

Here are some cool facts that not many people know:

- When a person cries take note of which eye produces the first tear. If it is the right eye this means they are tears of happiness. The left eye producing the first tear means pain or sorrow. If the tears flow from both eyes this means frustration.
- Want to win at "rock paper scissors"? Try asking your opponent a question directly before starting the game. Studies have shown they will throw scissors ninety percent of the time.

- No time to meditate or chill during your busy day? Try coloring in! A quick ten minutes concentrating on coloring will help you release anxiety and stress.
- Che gum if you are nervous. Our brains are tuned to recognize that if we are eating then we are not in danger. This allows you to relax and abandon the fight or flight response.
- When you are talking to someone speak into their right ear and touch them gently on their right forearm. This will increase the chance they will agree with you by fifty percent!

How to tell what people are thinking

Wouldn't it be great to read people's minds? What an advantage that would give you. Of course, we can't do this, but we can learn a great deal from other sources. Here are the best ways to read other people.

- Are you unsure if someone is watching you or checking you out? Try yawning and look around at them. If they are yawning too it means they were looking at you!
- When talking with someone try crossing your arms. If they mirror the action this indicates they are still interested in what you are saying.
- Do you want to spend time with someone you like but are not sure a date would be appropriate? Ask what their favorite movie is and then comment that you haven't seen it.

They will always say, "We should watch it" if they have any interest in you at all.
- When approaching someone check out their feet. If they only turn their torsos and their feet remain in a different direction you are not welcome. The same applies when you are in a conversation with someone. If their feet are facing another direction, they want the conversation to end.

Tips to help you form new relationships.

Romantic or otherwise our lives can be enriched by the right relationships. How do we break down the barriers and form a bond that will grow? Here are a few tips to help you make those connections.

- Do you think someone you are interested in has given you a false number? Repeat it back to them with one number wrong and see if they correct you.
- Do you want to get someone's number but don't want to ask for it? Get them to take a picture of you both and send it to you. This is also a great way to give your number without it seeming awkward. This tip is handy in crowded noisy places like a party or concert.
- Make sure your hands are always warm. Shaking hands with somebody who has warm palm makes the other person want to get along with you. Do not go too far as sweaty

palms are a definite no-no! Cold hands can indicate a cold personality and will give an immediate negative response.
- Women are more likely to ask questions they already know the answer to. Be honest or you risk looking like a fool!
- How do you know if the person you are with is right for you? The best relationship advice I have ever heard is this. "Be with someone who gives you the same sense of joy you experience when your food is coming to your favorite restaurant!"
- When you feel close to someone you will hear their voice in your head when you read their texts.

Just for fun!

Finally, here are a few fun facts that you can use to impress your friends!

- Try brushing your teeth or combing your hair with your opposite hand. This improves self-control.
- If you are struggling to stay awake have a hot drink followed by a cold one. Your brain will feel refreshed by the combination and help you stay alert.
- If you are experiencing anger, try drawing wavy lines on a piece of paper. Creating patterns will help you calm down.
- If you want a friend to carry your bag, engage them in conversation when you pass the bag to them. They will automatically accept it and carry it for you!

- If someone at work is about to say something derogative about you in a meeting sit next to them. It is a known fact that people find it hard to speak badly about someone who is in their proximity.
- The way you speak to your kids forms their inner voice. Think about how you remember your parent's voices at key times in your life. Your kids will do the same. Make sure they do not pick-up negative traits from you.
- Most of the problems in our lives are down to two key factors. Acting without proper thought and thinking without acting.
- School does not measure intelligence it simply tests your memory skills. You begin to learn skills for life once you have left formal education.
- Do you want to know who is connected in a group of people you don't know? Laugh at an amusing tale when you are in their company. The ones with the closest ties will make eye contact when sharing a laugh.

Remember that the biggest lie we tell ourselves is "I'm fine" Respect your own feelings and you will encourage others to do the same.

Chapter 16: The Difference between Persuasion and Manipulation

Seeing how individuals structure assessments, contentions, and display and incorporate realities into their psychological models is mission-basic in your capacity to persuade anyone to become tied up with a thought and afterward follow up on that thought. That is the embodiment of influence.

The distinction between influence and manipulation lies in:

1) The expectation behind your craving to convince that individual,

2) The honesty and straightforwardness of the procedure, and

3) The net advantage or effect on that individual

Manipulation suggests influence with the goal to track, control or think up the individual on the opposite side of the discussion into accomplishing something, thinking something, or becoming tied up with something that leaves them either hurt or without advantage.

It might likewise suggest that you are disguising a craving to move them to your perspective, such that it will profit you. What's more, if this advantage were uncovered, that disclosure would make the other individual far less open to your message since it would either:

- Demonstrate a solid inclination towards their absence of advantage in the trade,
- Demonstrate an ulterior thought process in the endeavor at influence, frequently determined by uneven advantage, or
- Some mix of both.

So, for instance, suppose I was selling someone a vehicle, and I had the entirety of my devices of influence and techniques. That individual strolled into my business, and it was evident, with a group of six children, they were searching for and truly required a family-sized, reasonable vehicle.

In any case, I at that point utilized the entirety of my powerful capacities to persuade the parent that he shouldn't purchase a little van yet rather a two-seater convertible to recover his childhood, and in doing as such, show his kids that it is so essential to remain consistent with their energetic standards, realizing beyond any doubt that I would make double the commission on that vehicle and it was totally unsatisfactory for them.

That is manipulation.

Presently, imagine a scenario where that equivalent parent came into my business with a similar six children and said to me, "Man, I simply need to blow some money. I should purchase a six-setter. I know it's totally silly, and I truly can't legitimize this. However, I'm only jonesing for the two-seater convertible?"

Also, imagine a scenario in which I then I utilized my convincing capacities to gradually and deliberately spread out a discussion and a lot of realities that drove this parent to comprehend the certifiable advantage of acquiring the more moderate and appropriate family vehicle.

That is influence, not manipulation.

Since I utilized a similar arrangement of aptitudes to persuade someone to accomplish something that I truly accepted was to their greatest advantage, rather than persuading them to accomplish something that I was almost certain was not to their greatest advantage – and likely was in effect not exactly honest with at any rate some portion of what I was discussing.

At last, influence methodologies, apparatuses, and a comprehension of how to introduce realities, contentions, and communications such that is bound to get someone on the opposite side of the discussion to become tied up with your perspective are basically about influence.

It's the hidden expectation, the net advantage, and the veracity with which you breathe life into this tool kit that makes the contrast among influence and manipulation.

The distinction between influence and manipulation has been a subject of discussion for truly a huge number of years. In old Greece, during the fourth century BC, the dad of influence, Aristotle, restricted a gathering of educators known as the Sophists. The Sophists gave guidance in different controls yet got notorious for their educating of talk. Aristotle conflicted with the Sophists over the way that they couldn't have cared less about truth yet would advance any thought for an expense. Aristotle stated that the Sophists were taking part in manipulation since they purposefully misdirected individuals and caused hurt.

Why Persuasion Is Good

To precisely perceive the distinction between influence and manipulation, it is fundamental to comprehend the morals that undergird influence. There are some correspondence scholars who have proclaimed that influence is "morally impartial. In other words, that influence is neither acceptable nor terrible, however simply a fair-minded procedure. I don't acknowledge this position. I would fight that the Aristotelian perspective that influence isn't nonpartisan, however honorable, is right. Influence is intrinsically acceptable in light of the fact that it is one of the essential methods through which truth gets known. Through the influential strategy, a thought is advanced with proof, and an individual is permitted to decide to either acknowledge or dismiss that powerful intrigue openly. Influence does, without a doubt, include moving individuals to a position they don't right now hold, however not by asking or persuading. Rather, it includes cautious planning, the best possible encircling of contentions, the introduction of distinctive supporting proof, and the push to locate the right passionate match with your crowd.

The conviction that influence is a fair and powerful method for landing at truth is seen by the way that it is the reason for present-day financial aspects, directing practices, and the lawful framework. What's more, influence is additionally the establishment of majority rule government. Majority rules systems utilize attentive moral influence at whatever point they choose pioneers, set up laws, or attempt to ensure their residents. Indeed, even the individuals who become alarmed with the thought of influence can't get away from it. Influence is imbued inside human correspondence. When imparting, individuals both deliberately and unexpectedly advance certain convictions and practices. Thus, influence doesn't involve decisions; it is innate in social connection. Indeed, it is so inescapable in human correspondence that, on occasion, it turns out to be practically undetectable. The supposed individuals' callings – legislative issues, law, social work, advising, business the board, promoting, deals, advertising, and the service – should be called influence callings.

At its center, influence is the quest for truth. It is through the influence that positive change happens. For instance, influential messages have been logically demonstrated to incite secondary school understudies to abstain from smoking, increment lifesaving blood gifts, and keep youth from joining packs. Influence helps manufacture harmony understandings between countries. Influence assists open with increasing shut social orders. Influence is pivotal to the gathering pledges endeavors of good cause and generous associations. Influence persuades drivers to lock in when driving or to forgo driving when they've had a couple of such a large number of beverages. Influence is utilized to persuade a drunkard or medication subordinate relative to look for proficient assistance. Influence is the manner by which the mentor of a dark horse group moves the players to give it their everything. Influence is an apparatus utilized by guardians to ask kids not to acknowledge rides from outsiders or to permit anybody to contact them such that feels awkward. So, influence is the foundation of various positive, pro social attempts. Next to no of the decency that we find on the planet could be practiced without influence.

However, the integrity of influence and the way that it is implanted inside human instinct isn't what causes individuals' concern. What causes nervousness if the debasement of influence. Undoubtedly, when influence is mutilated, it can get manipulative, which is perilous. Through manipulation, scalawags, religion pioneers, and tyrants have mishandled, oppressed, and even slaughtered millions. In any case, as unfavorable as manipulation may be, it ought to never be mistaken for influence. Manipulation is the corruption of influence. It isn't worried about truth but instead double-dealing. Aristotle remarked on this in his acclaimed work, Rhetoric when he accentuated, "a maltreatment of the explanatory workforce can work extraordinary evil, a similar charge can be brought against every beneficial thing spare righteousness itself, and particularly against the most helpful things, for example, quality, wellbeing, riches, and military aptitude. Properly utilized, they work the best gift; and wrongly utilized, they work the best damage.

Therefore, the appropriate inquiry is how you might recognize influence and manipulation? Coming up next are the three clear, yet dependable ways that you can break down if a message is manipulative.

1. Intention

The aim is an essential factor in deciding whether a solicitation is manipulative. In the event that individual endeavors to exhibit a thought or conduct that isn't to the greatest advantage of another, they are participating in manipulation. Unfortunately, this is very normal. Individuals habitually fall into the snare of manhandling others in the quest for what they want. One of the underlying drivers of this Machiavellian point of view isn't seeing others with equity. The famous scholar Immanuel Kant expounded on this attitude when he recommended that the central statute of ethical quality is regarding an individual as a person and not as a thing.

2. Withholding Truth

Manipulation includes misshaping or retaining truth. Regularly, this is seen through overstating the upsides of conduct, thought, or item. It was this type of manipulation that incited the expression Caveat Emptor, which is Latin for "Purchaser Beware," to get predominant. The expression was especially far-reaching during those chronicled periods when there was little responsibility for venders. The maxim was an admonition to potential purchasers to be suspicious of those selling merchandise, and to ensure that they confirmed, before making a buy, that the nature of the item was indistinguishable from the cases made by the dealer. Indeed, even today, a great many people have encountered being told about the highlights or advantages of an item or administration, and afterward, in the wake of obtaining it understood that they had been misdirected. This isn't right, as something besides genuine portrayal is conspicuous manipulation.

3. Coercion

The pressure is the third and most clear segment of a manipulative intrigue. It is the expulsion of free decision, the final proposal – do it, or something bad might happen. Interestingly, influence includes impact, however, never power. A characterizing normal for influence is a free decision. At some level, the individual must be fit for tolerating or dismissing the position that has been encouraged by the person in question. Along these lines, a greeting that one can't state no to isn't powerful in nature yet is coercive and as needs are manipulative.

There is a huge contrast between influence and manipulation. Influence propels the situation of all included. It is a prosaically try that aides the recipient of a message in tolerating truth. Interestingly, a manipulative intrigue is one that, whenever embraced, will adversely affect another. Manipulation is ethically off base and, at last counterproductive to the interests of all included. The deliberate utilization of misdirecting impact strategies... at last, it turns into a mentally and monetarily self-harming process. In this manner, through a precise and powerful comprehension of both the rightness of influence and the three essential components of manipulation, you will be better ready to convince others morally and shield yourself from manipulative solicitations.

The most effective method to develop your influencing skills

We frequently need to convince and impact those over whom we have no genuine position. The inquiry is how to do this in a viable and unpretentious manner?

An inconspicuous, compassionate methodology is suggested as opposed to a more straightforward or powerful style

Persuasion requires empathy

Give the other party the feeling that you have met them midway or further

An inconspicuous, compassionate methodology is suggested as opposed to a more straightforward or powerful style.

Chapter 17: Moral and Earn Respect

It is almost impossible to separate the leader from those he leads. After all, no leader exists in isolation. Indeed, of the most difficult and complex aspects of leadership in inspiring feelings of willingness and capability in those who are being led. It is vital to not overlook the human element of success in any given plan. Both Sun Tzu and Machiavelli offered various insights into the human aspects of leadership. This phase contains a distillation of their key ideas and ways of applying them in the modern context. The phase draws ideas from various sections of both The Art of War and The Prince.

The Human Element

A common mistake when leaders devise and attempt to execute strategic plans is overlooking a vital part of the process - the human element. Humans are often overlooked as part of the process of strategic thought as it is assumed, they will act in a certain way regardless. This is a huge mistake. The morale, motivation and other factors relevant to the people being led can be huge influences on how successful or otherwise any given plan is in reality.

Bad planners see the role of humans within strategy as being simpler than it actually is. People mistakenly think that if a person has the right skills and is in the right situation, they will succeed. This is actually forgetting a vital piece of the puzzle. While it is true that the person does need to have the right skills for the environment in which they will work, their internal state is also a key component. People can have all the skills their work needs, but, if they don't feel motivated to put in effort, it is all for nothing.

Human beings are too complex to ever fully 'map out' and the almost infinite variations that can take place in plans as a result of the people carrying them out can be overwhelming. However, it is always important to at least attempt to understand how different human factors can impact plans. It is better to have a rough idea of something complex than no idea whatsoever.

Comparative States

Usually, there are various ways in which you can assess the people under your control as a collective group. For example, you may lead a team of ten people. Within that team, six are average workers, two are slow workers and two are fast workers. Overall, you could say that this team averaged out to being at a standard pace. Other areas in which your people can be assessed include their levels of skill, levels of motivation, years of experience within the company and any other measure which seems relevant to the operation taking place.

While it is undoubtedly useful to measure the people you are leading, it is also important to compare this to the human element of your competitor. For example, let's say your company and a competing company are launching a similar product within the same region. By preparing the skill level of your sales teams comparatively, the motivation within the teams and the general morale, it may emerge that one company has a human advantage over their competing rival.

If you are comparing the human aspect of two entities, it is vital to compare them in a valid way. For example, if you are measuring the relative skillsets, of the teams, you would want to be sure the comparison is based on comparable measures. Someone who has years of experience in programming is obviously a different prospect to someone who holds a certificate in a programming language but lacks on the job experience. It is therefore vital that any system of measurement you devise allows for variations such as the amount of experience within a particular area.

Understand that comparisons are not perfect. Business is not carried out on paper. Sports is a clear illustration of this concept. Often, the team which is the much better prospect on paper ends up losing to a lesser team. Business is no different. A company that seems to be in a great position on paper can end up performing worse than a seemingly weaker competitor. Comparing any aspect of business is imperfect and incomplete - comparing an element as unpredictable and complex as humans are doubly so.

Loyalty & Discipline

Sun Tzu was keen to emphasize in the Art of War the importance of taking a different approach to discipline of those you lead depending on the nature of your relationship with them. It is taught that discipline can only be implemented once the people that are being led feel genuine loyalty to a leader. If a leader tries to implement discipline too early then it will work against them and harm the chances of loyalty. If people are loyal, though, they must be disciplined in order for their loyalty to be sustained.

The concept of differing levels of discipline can be applied in the modern corporate context. When taking over a team for the first time, a new leader often eases back on implementing their rules and regulations too strictly until the team has unified and people feel united with one another. If the leader attempts to implement discipline too early then it ruins the chances of team cohesion. After a while, however, it is vital for the discipline to be in place in order for the team to function smoothly.

One of the arts of leadership is to strike the balance between discipline and loyalty at any given time. Depending on the nature of the situation and the people being disciplined, it may be better to discipline too strongly or too weakly. Generally speaking, it is better to discipline too strongly than too weakly, as this is more likely to lead to a leader being feared.

Respect and Fear

Machiavelli stated in The Prince that leaders are able to rule through either respect or fear. A people's respect can be fickle and difficult to rely upon, whereas Machiavelli felt that fear was a reliable predictor of compliance with a leader's wishes. Machiavelli therefore stated it was better to be feared than anything else as this was the only way of ensuring loyalty and compliance from the people.

Sun Tzu was keen to emphasize that a leader must earn the respect of the people they led. He stated that this could only come through being a wise and decisive leader and always valuing the efforts of troops in any given situation. Sun Tzu was keen to emphasize that conflict should only be entered into when victory could be assured and this belief was a key to keeping morale up and troops onside.

This principle is very relevant for the modern leader. Too many leaders of the contemporary time are mistaken in thinking that notions of loyalty or ethics will always keep morale up and workers loyal. Instead, it is vital that a leader is feared. This can only be achieved by being unafraid to take harsh action to ensure wishes are complied with. Any dissent, or signs of dissent, must be crushed without hesitation.

Morale as Advisor

Sun Tzu was keen to state that the comparative morale of two sets of troops in a conflict could even be used as a valuable way of making decisions. Sun Tzu advocated delaying certain maneuvers until a time when your own troops were in higher spirits and fighting with more commitment than the other side. Sun Tzu felt strongly about this to stress that it could make the difference between victory and failure.

With this knowledge in mind, the modern leader should always seek to assess the levels of motivation and morale present in the organizations of competitors. Times of low competitive morale are ideal times to launch maneuvers and aim to gain strategic ground. Some leaders aim to take this principle to its logical conclusion and manipulate and influence the morale of both sides as per the strategic requirement of the time. This can be achieved through the manipulative release of information to influence perception. This is a powerful combination of the principle of Machiavellian psychological manipulation and Sun Tzu's use of morale and motivation as a guide to decision making.

Never Overlook

It is easy to get wrapped up with the complex strategic frameworks and Art of War comparative measures that form part of the equation of victory. However, the wisest leaders never lose sight of the fact that all plans are carried out by people. The beliefs and mentalities of the people in an organization are a direct determinant of that organization's outcomes. People can be influenced and failing to do so is overlooking a key element of the Art of War. Finally, it is vital to remember that the motivation of people should never be viewed in isolation, but rather as a piece of a broader strategic puzzle.

Chapter 18: Strategies to Improve Your Mental Toughness

This is the part of the where we tie everything together and connect the dots back to mental toughness. Everything we've talked about so far is one small part of the mental toughness mindset, so learning how to implement all of it will give you the complete picture. Each strategy will also include a simple action step for you to do so that you're not just reading about how to improve your mental toughness—you're actually doing it.

Mental toughness gives you the ability to tune your responses and react in ways that help you move forward. It also makes you more aware of all the opportunities that you may have missed in the past as a result of the blinders that you put on when life gets hard. It's more than a mindset; it's a lifestyle. In truth, it's about to become your lifestyle.

Putting Everything Together

This will be a bit of a recap of everything we've covered so far so that you know exactly what your next steps should be. It's easy enough to read about how to be mentally tough, but you probably need a little guidance to get started applying all that knowledge to your life.

Do yourself a favor and get a journal or even a notebook so that you can track your progress. Every time you make an effort to get out of your comfort zone, develop a habit, conquer stress, practice being resilient and disciplined, and prepare for a challenge, write it down. Whenever you rely on mental toughness to get you through something, take note of it. Even when you feel like you failed to be mentally tough, write that down, too, and ask yourself why you weren't able to apply toughness to the situation. This isn't for anyone's eyes but your own, so be honest and open. You won't become mentally tough overnight. If it was that easy, you wouldn't have to read a guide about it. It's going to take time and practice, and a journal is a way for you to visually see the steps you've taken and the progress you've made.

So, let's take a look at the attitudes and actions you need to have and take in order to build up your mental toughness.

Get Out of Your Comfort Zone

We don't need to go over all of that again, but if you need a quick reminder of what exactly comfort zones are and how you can tell if you're in one, skim that section before moving on.

We covered how to get out of your comfort zone first because it might just be the most important step. You'll never learn mental toughness if you never have to rely on it, and you won't have to in your comfort zone. If you skip this step, you might as well skip everything else because it won't do you any good. Cut the cord, burn those bridges, take the leap, and leave your comfort zones far behind. Nothing life-changing will ever happen in there because life never changes.

That's another thing you need to remember and take to heart—change is good. It's better than godwit's essential. You'll never find out your true potential if you stay the same from the time you're born until you die. The moment you break away from your comfort zone is when you'll discover yourself. Nothing in your life will change if you don't change first, and the only way to do so is to get away from your old life and habits.

Action Step: Commit to doing one thing that scares you every day. That's right every single day. For at least a week. It can be as small as trying a new food or as big as speaking up in a meeting. Whenever you're in a situation that kicks up your fight-or-flight reflex, choose fight. It's going to be nerve-wracking at first, but that's the point. Once you start to get comfortable with fear and the feeling of apprehension that goes along with it, you'll realize that it's not so bad after all. There's no better way to learn how to master your fear than to run toward it.

Develop Habits without Waiting for Motivation

Hopefully, you realize by now that motivation is a sham. If you haven't, I challenge you to try to stay motivated for an entire day while doing something you don't find fun. Time waits for no one, so don't waste it trying to find motivation that just isn't going to come. In order to use your time and brain power wisely, you need habits.

You learned why your brain likes habits and how to develop them, so we won't go over all of that again. In short, your brain wants to have the easiest job possible, so it evaluates your routines, condenses repeated ones into automatic habits, and moves on to bigger and more taxing things.

That's one of the biggest secrets of mental toughness—learning how to automate certain processes so that you can focus on situations that require more attention and quick thinking. When your brain is bogged down, trying to make decisions about the little things, you have less power to devote to more pressing matters. In essence, that's why habits are important.

There's a lot of advice you'll find out there about the best ways to build habits, but it's genuinely a simple process. Do something repeatedly, then reward yourself for doing it. Presto, you've just created a habit! It can be a little tougher if you're trying to replace a bad habit with a more positive one, but it follows the same principle. Tell your brain to do something, convince it that it's worth the effort, and your brain will want to do it all the time.

Action Step: Pick one habit that you think will help you live a more fulfilling life. It can be related to work or your personal life. Furthermore, it can either be a significant change to your routine or a small addition to your day. It just has to mean something to you. Don't forget to implement the cue-action-reward cycle. Pick a cue, decide on an action, then have a reward ready when you complete that action.

If you're keeping a journal, track your progress. Challenge yourself to see how many days in a row you can follow through. If you forget or miss a day, put a nice big red X next to the date, not as a punishment but as a visual reminder. You don't want to see red Xs, so do everything you can to stick with your developing habit. When you get to the end of the month, congratulate yourself and keep on going. Pick up another habit if you think you can handle it. Lifestyles are built one habit at a time, so take that first step.

Embrace Good Stress and Manage Bad Stress

This is the aspect of mental toughness that can be the most confusing. We either can't tell the difference between good stress and bad stress or don't use good stress effectively, or we let bad stress cause us to freeze in our tracks. Some people can handle stress better than others, but that's because they've learned how to. Once you learn that, you'll find out that life isn't so difficult after all.

The best strategy for any kind of stress is to control it. Accepting a lack of control when it comes to stressors, but the stress itself is entirely within your power. It comes from within you, after all.

Don't make the mistake of thinking that all your stress will disappear when you become mentally tough. The truth is that it will always be there. The difference is that it won't have mastery over you anymore. When you can channel good stress into your work and use it to propel you forward, you succeed. When you can recognize where bad stress originates from and work to overcome it instead of letting it overcome you, you win.

Action Step: Chances are, you encounter a stressful situation every day. The next time that happens, do two things. First, recognize whether it's good stress or bad stress. Then, if it's good stress, find a way to use it to help you. If it's bad stress, realize that you don't control the situation, only your actions. Although you may have stopped everything and let the stress get you down or make you panic in the past, you're now going to wave hi to it and continue walking. You'll acknowledge that it's there, but you won't give it any more thought.

Be Resilient and Cultivate Discipline

These are bundled into one because they build off each other. Resilience improves discipline, and discipline improves resilience. It's that simple. Of course, in practice, it's not that easy.

How much resilience do we normally need to get through the day? There's no set amount, but we apply minimal resilience to our day-to-day activities on average. The only time we call on it is when we're in a jam and need extra help. This is why we find it so difficult to be resilient—we don't do it often enough. The same goes for discipline.

We already talked about how to be more disciplined and resilient, but what we didn't explore was how to be more of each more often. This means using resilience and discipline all the time, not just when you think you need them. It's like a dress rehearsal, but for mental toughness. Practice enough times, and you'll be ready when you really need it.

Action Step: For every small challenge that crops up during the day, call on all the resilience you can muster. Whether you spill coffee on your clothes, show up late, or burn dinner, it doesn't matter. You're going to bounce back. You're not going to say, "Well it's going to be one of those days" because it isn't. It's a new day, unlike any other.

Every chance you get to be disciplined, do it with all your heart. If you're pushing to finish the last bit of a project, avoiding the candy machine, or trying to have more patience with the kids, do it fully and completely. Work until you're done, stay away from temptation, and remind yourself why you're going what you're doing. Discipline isn't available in a finite amount. It gets stronger the more you use it.

Chapter 19: Be Calm and Strong in Every Situation

In many respects, everything in this phase can be considered a "strength" that contributes to mental toughness. In addition, of course, there are those strengths (capabilities and traits) that are your own unique advantages and personal assets, things that make you singularly effective. But before we look at those kinds of strengths, we'll talk about strength in its other meaning.

"Strength" can refer to the amount of stress, pressure, strain, or force that something (or someone) can withstand – or offer against something else. That relates to durability, endurance, and power. We have already talked about flexibility (and the willingness to change) as being one component of that type of strength, that is, of the ability to withstand stress.

It must be noted that true strength of this kind, being strong mentally, is not the same as putting on a show of strength. The person who only makes an outward display of strength may be able to appear strong on days when there is no stress. However, the moment that stress increases and becomes overwhelming, that external show of strength breaks down.

On the other hand, a person who has genuine internal strength and isn't wasting effort on projecting an appearance of strength is able to handle a crisis and stress better. There is mental capacity to spare when it isn't wasted on maintaining an act or defending an image.

There is a saying, "Still waters run deep." Strength that runs deep below the surface reveals itself in the face of adversity and stress. But strength that is projected onto the surface evaporates as soon as stress is applied to that superficial image.

Mental toughness is about inner strength. It's not about huge muscles, chiseled biceps, or the biggest guns. As Theodore Roosevelt, the longest serving American President and mentally tough despite ill health and being crippled by polio, once said, "Speak softly and carry a big stick." While tin-pot dictators may flex their muscles with military parades, this is not what we mean by the kind of strength that contributes to mental toughness.

When someone starts trying to show off how strong they are, that is usually a sure sign that important weaknesses are being masked and that there isn't any real strength there. Generally, the most powerful people are also the most reserved about displaying their power. Humility has its own kind of strength to add into the mix.

The strength of mental toughness isn't about brute strength or aggression. Someone who is typically quick to anger and ready to throw a punch or express disagreement through physical force reveals a limited internal strength. That kind of behavior is driven more by ego preservation or by one of the many fears that reside in the primal part of the brain.

While tin-pot dictators everywhere in the world have come and gone, the quiet, understated strength of mentally tough leaders like Martin Luther King and Mahatma Gandhi, who stood up against overwhelming forces to change history, continue to inspire millions to their causes. Brute strength may put a dictator ahead of the game at first, but eventually every one of them, from Stalin to Hitler, to Pol Pot and Idi Amin, all have ended up on the ash heap of history.

So, where does that powerful inner strength come from? That kind of inner strength and mental toughness comes from having the confidence of knowing who you are, what you believe (your perspective), and your own personal strengths – and being able to rely on them.

For the moment, set aside your concerns for your weaknesses. Instead, this is about identifying what your strengths are, doing more of them, building them up, and buttressing your mental toughness with them. When you know you have a particular strength, talent, or capability that you can rely on, it provides you not only with a reserve of confidence and power to draw from when you need to be mentally tough, but also specific capabilities you can call upon in situations of stress or crisis. In other words, knowing your own personal "strengths" contributes to your inner strength.

To identify your own personal "strengths," don't just write a list of what you think they are or of things that you think you're good at. You don't want a list of what you automatically think of, and you don't want to overstate or underestimate your abilities either.

Instead, to dig deeper and assess your strengths more accurately, look back to times you overcame challenges, when you "won" at something. Perhaps you got a promotion at work because you did your job exceptionally well. Were you accepted into university because you excelled academically? Maybe you built a birdhouse. Make a list of things you consider victories or accomplishments. List things you were praised for, rewarded for, felt good about, and so on. Look for times you vanquished obstacles, and look at what it took to get there. Also, look at the desires you've had in your life, and list the ones you've achieved – a hobby, a family, a house, a car, a good job, an education.

Now comes the important part of the exercise. Dig into each victory or accomplishment on your list and look for the specific underlying strengths and abilities you had to demonstrate to achieve it. What did you do differently from situations where you (or others) didn't succeed? You'll find patterns emerging. There will also be things so natural and easy for you that you take them for granted. Maybe you are really good at persuading skeptics face-to-face. It could be that you produce outstanding work when you spend extra time organizing it beforehand. You'll be surprised by the strengths you have that you never even realized were there.

Use that list to make better choices, doing what is most aligned with your personal strengths. It might suggest new directions you hadn't thought of before. Working from your strengths will always be more powerful, moving you forward faster than struggling through weaknesses. It'll waste less mental resources, and it'll keep you in your mental toughness zone.

Self-awareness

Self-awareness goes hand in hand with having mental strength and toughness. It's hard to imagine someone without self-knowledge or self-awareness as being mentally tough.

This guide won't focus on understanding your personal strengths so much as just becoming more self-aware generally, and on understanding your own way of getting in and out of difficulties. Ultimately, you need to understand as much as you can about yourself, your strengths, and weaknesses, if you are going to be mentally tough.

Self-awareness normally comes with age, wisdom, and experience, but you don't have to wait, if you learn the art of observation and reflection. The kind of self-awareness that normally takes a lifetime of experiences to acquire can be yours with observation and reflection.

A regular practice of reflection is equally valuable (even crucial) for gaining self-awareness.

There is another useful and easy technique for self-reflection that you can use to better understand yourself (or any situation). You can use it to uncover hidden issues, unexpected connections between things, and hidden motives. Do this exercise on your own in writing or partner up with another person who can ask the questions. It's a good technique to add to your repertoire of journaling exercises.

The exercise uses a framework of "Why?" questions. The answers gradually reveal what isn't readily apparent on the surface, including contradictions.

Identify an issue about yourself that you want to understand better, and start asking, "Why?" Each time you have an answer, ask "Why?" of that answer, creating a chain of questions and answers.

1. Why?
2. Why?
3. Why?
4. Why?
5. Why?

Each time you ask "Why?" you peel away another layer to reveal another set of hidden causes until you find a root cause. Keep going until you feel you've exhausted the issue by experiencing an "Aha!" or just reaching the bottom of the issue.

For example, perhaps you just paid a regular bill late again, even though you had the money. You could start by asking yourself, "I paid this bill late. Why?" and quietly allowing an answer to arise from within. If the answer is "I don't like paying that bill," the next question naturally is, "Why don't I like paying this bill?" Perhaps the answer is, "I feel that I might need that money for an emergency." That leads to the next question, "Why do I feel I'll need money for an emergency?" Any number of answers could emerge from that, leading to the next question, and so forth.

By the time you have get to the bottom of the matter; you realize you need a certain amount of financial cushion to feel safe. In other words, you have been paying that bill late because paying it arouses a feeling of insecurity instilled by a childhood of poverty. Seeing all the elements of the issue laid out so clearly makes it easier to understand (and forgive you for). A solution might also become obvious, just from doing the exercise, as in the next example.

A close friend's son was once suspended for cheating in school. His parents were livid and confused. Things weren't progressing toward a solution, so they asked me to help. I knew the boy to be intelligent, sharp witted, and quick to pick up things. Together, we went through the Why? Questions, and found the root problem within an hour, plain to see.

It turned out he'd been getting bad headaches and hadn't been able to keep up with his usual workload. He hadn't wanted to worry his parents, or let them down, so he started to get help from friends. One thing led to another, and he got caught. Within a week of going through the exercise, his eyes were checked, and corrective lenses prescribed. Within six weeks, he was back at the top of his class.

Doing the Why? Exercise can not only help identify solutions for problems, it can give you a lot of insight into yourself. In particular, it can really help you understand how you find yourself having problems with undesirable consequences.

Conclusion

It is not facile to read people and especially quickly. But when you are surrounded by manipulative people all around and want to read them and take correct decisions, it becomes imperative for you to analyze, read and take decisions accordingly. Anyone can read people and has the ability to do it, but you should know what to look for first. The basic things to observe while analyzing people are their posture, movements, gestures, tone, expressions and eye contact.

It is not imperative to read minds. You just need to pay heed to these details to understand what is going in his mind. In fact, by noticing all this you can even assess a person when you meet him for the first time. Few people are like open books and easy to read but there are few which are very difficult to understand and read. But if you sharpen your skills and read the points below, I am sure you would become completely versed in analyzing and reading people in a speedway-

1) Create a baseline- There are many people who would regularly clear their throat, look at the floor, scratch their head, put their hands-on mouth, etc. First, you need to establish a baseline about the person by seeing what his normal behavior is. It would be bad on your side if you feel that a person is getting nervous or lying if

he is not maintaining eye contact. First, check his normal behavior if he normally as well does that, maybe it is the lack of confidence. So, you should not hurry while judging them, take some time and observe their regular behavior first.

2) Observe body language signs- The first thing that you should see is their appearance. See if they are wearing a shirt and shoes, a suit which shows that they are dressed formally and indicates ambition. If they are wearing jeans and shoes it shows that they like being comfortable and casual. Wearing any pendant of god might show they are spiritual. So, it is vital for you to first notice their physical appearance.

Secondly, check on their posture. You should check on the way they walk, they sit and talk. This would depict that they are confident enough or give a sign of low self-esteem. So, the time they enter check how they come and with what posture they sit.

Thirdly, see their physical movements. Observe if they are leaning too much, how they are sitting, lip biting or hiding hand or putting them in the pocket. This will show if they are nervous, confident or aggressive.

3) Facial Expressions- Another substantial thing to see his facial expressions as you can easily read them. If someone has deep frown lines it means that the person is worried or thinking too much. If you see someone clenching their jaw or teeth it means

that they are tensed. Also, if they press their fingers every now and then, that as well shows that they are nervous or anxious.

4) Listen to your gut feeling- It is something other than logic. Here you need to use your intuition and then judge the person. Intuition lets you see further than other things. Always listen to your gut feeling when you meet someone for the first time. Intuition is something that occurs when you meet someone for the first time and you can trust it. Also, if you get Goosebumps after meeting someone, it means that person has inspired you a lot and maybe is a positive sign.

Thus, these were few basic points which should be kept in mind when you are trying to read people and it would help you a lot as these are the basic points. It has already been proven that 55% of the information we can fetch a person by non-verbal communication only. These are a few signals which people send us without even knowing it and you have to get hold of those signals.